Praise for *Pissed Off*

"Michael Thornton is not as pissed off as he says. Switched on might be a better way of putting it. This book claims to be full of gripes and Thornton is surely entitled to a few of those. But is also replete with astute observations and devastating insights. It loves life and is peeved by the narrow-minded and ungenerous who spoil the fun. Thornton is great fireside company as you shelter from the storm."
— Michael McGirr, author of *Books that Saved My Life*

"Often, when you ask someone how they are, they'll say, 'I can't complain'. That's not Michael Thornton. He can complain, and when he does, the results are magnificent."
— Tony Moclair, Overnights, 3AW

"Who knew a list could be so much fun? But don't be misled -- there is much serious and valuable thought in Pissed Off, as well as laughs, as Michael Thornton harrumps his way through a heartless world."
— James Button, author of *Speechless*

"You made me laugh, bemused, self evaluate, groan and cynically assess myself. I loved every bit of It. Well done for connecting humanity with humility."
— Michael's chiropractor

"It's funny, satirical, has a good dash of pathos and beats "Grumpy Old Women" hands down. Whiplash from nodding agreement with many of Thornton's gripes, is a risk. The author's life is revealed in and between the lines. The reader's age may be only one of many factors which determine how amusing this book is. Thankfully, No. 70 (castrating lambs with one's teeth) is no longer practised. I think we all threaten to write a book like this at some stage. May No. 2478 come true for you, Mr Thornton."
— Jessie Keyssecker, author of *Nobody Chews an Oyster*

"Thornton has written a book filled with nostalgia, irony and satire that brings a wry grin of agreement and a chuckle of recognition. He does so with beautifully crafted observations of us."
— Kit Adam, Author of *A Climate of Change*

"With great trepidation, I opened this new book by Michael Thornton, and was so surprised to find pages and pages of gripes I found myself heartily endorsing. (There were a few I could take issue with you Michael)
  This is the perfect book for conversation starters. Many stand out. *'petrol companies which make service stations lift fuel prices when it is the same petrol in their underground tank which they sold yesterday'* (I will never get it either). *'church leaders who say they would go to jail before reporting a confessing paedophile.'* I loved the repeat of *'nothing to see here'*. However, I was left hanging in mid-air over the cheque signing incident.....what happened here?
  I totally agree with being peeved off with the phrase, *'jump on line'*....nobody jumps anywhere. So many topics are covered from politicians to reading instruction manuals. This makes it the perfect gift or coffee table edition to any home.
  Two peeves that stand out are (i) the thought *'we need how to learn to be unhappy'* and (ii) *'the undiscussed correlation between violence on the screen and violence in society at large.'*
  Congratulations Michael, on a brilliant concept book. I am sure it will be a best seller."
— Judith Flitcroft, author of *Walk Back in Time*

"A witty thought-provoking and often nostalgic read. The ultimate coffee-table edition for stimulating conversation."
— Vivian Waring, author of *When Tears Ran Dry*.

PISSED OFF

3,300 Baby Boomer Gripes

Michael Thornton

Published in Australia by Sid Harta Books & Print Pty Ltd,
ABN: 34632585293
23 Stirling Crescent, Glen Waverley, Victoria 3150 Australia
Telephone: +61 3 9560 9920, Facsimile: +61 3 9545 1742
E-mail: author@sidharta.com.au

First published in Australia 2021
This edition published 2021
Copyright © Michael Thornton 2021
Cover design, typesetting: WorkingType (www.workingtype.com.au)

The right of Michael Thornton to be identified as the Author of the Work has been asserted in accordance with the Copyright, Designs and Patents Act 1988.

All rights reserved. No part of this publication may be reproduced, stored in a retrieval system, or transmitted, in any form or by any means without the prior written permission of the publisher, nor be otherwise circulated in any form of binding or cover other than that in which it is published and without a similar condition being imposed on the subsequent purchaser.

This book is a work of satire.

This Manuscript is the property of the author. It should not under any intentions be copied or reproduced without copyright allowance. Nor should the person engaged with the document change the content for their personal gain.

Thornton, Michael
Pissed Off
ISBN: 978-1-925707-49-6
pp398

About the Author

One-time jackaroo Michael Thornton describes himself as 'retired' or 'author', depending on who's asking. He's worked in fundraising, although ever since his years in journalism, writing has been a foremost passion. He lives in Melbourne with his partner, Kass.

Books by Michael Thornton
Our First President
JACKAROO
*27 Days A Pilgrim on the
Camino de Santiago de Compostela*

For Kass

CONTENTS

About The Author	iii
Contents	vi
Introduction	1
13 Leading Pissers	3
A Raft of Pissers (1)	6
Brotherly Love	76
Financial Woes	77
Millennials	81
Supermarkets (1)	82
Driving (1)	85
Dating	87
Letter to Bus Company	89
Random Pissers	91
Sexism / Ageism / Racism (1)	93
Computer Speak	95
Sexism, Ageism, Racism (2)	98
Hard Quiz	99
Life's Dreads	101
Great Australian	103

Role Model	106
Telemarketing	107
Petrol Head Daughter	109
School Scandal	110
Important Advice	112
Retirement	113
Opinion Polls	115
Uncrickety	116
Politics	118
Weight Loss	120
Instructions	121
Bull Ring	123
Random Pissers (1)	125
Retail Staff	127
Why I Hate... [Insert Name]	128
Ripped Off	130
Random Pissers (2)	131
Dreaded Words	133
South Sudanese	134
Lies, Lies, Lies	136
Charitable Intents	137
Book Borrowings	139
Putting On The Mozz	141
Life's Little Protests	142
Quiz	144
Gifts	146
Worries	147
Believe it or Not	149

A Raft of Pissers (2)	151
School Scandal (2)	238
Things I Wish I'd Known	239
Taxpayer Angst	245
I Failed	246
Bucket List	248
Messy Business	250
Supermarkets (2)	252
Pay Tv	254
Sign Language	256
Driving (2)	257
Grammar	259
Woke & Bespoke	261
Rules	262
Yes, Minister	264
Aged Poo!	265
Unparliamentary	267
Love Languages	269
Dementia (1)	271
Walking The Camino	272
Reunions & Funerals	274
Concussion	276
Glen Campbell	278
Gambling	280
Crossing the Equator	282
Health Scare	284
Dementia (2)	286
Bullying	287

Good Old Tv	289
Job Applications	291
Don't Mess with Staff	293
Fishy Tale	294
Truly?	296
A Raft of Pissers (3)	304
Ace Engineer	351
Caught Short	352
Letting Go	354
Jonathon	355
Dead Bosses	357
What are the Odds?	359
All Isn't Fine	361
No Number, No Name	363
Vocation	364
Coronavirus Pandemic	366
The Good	367
The Bad	370
The Funny	378
Epilogue	381
Feedback	384
Leftovers	385

INTRODUCTION

I've turned seventy-one. It qualifies me to be a grumpy old fart. Who says? I say.

1 Doesn't it piss you off, the way it does me, how otherwise intelligent folk say *'amount of people?'* Number is for things we can count, like people. Amount is for things we can't count, like all of the crap in our lives.

2 Ditto 'fewer' and 'less': fewer people, less crap. Even prime ministers get these wrong, not to mention inarticulate sporting commentators. Grrr!

3 Then there is 'I' and 'me.' It's 'John and I' at the *start* of a sentence; 'John and me' at the *end*. Think about it. John and I each took a shovel. Janice gave it to John and me, not to I.

It's not only grammar. Drivers, supermarkets and constantly being screwed piss me off.

Before compiling this collection, I had no idea how

much angst welled inside me. Yet, putting fingers to keyboard has shown how much of day-to-day life pisses me off. I hope that committing your list to tablet will help you to let go of your frustrations, too.

Be gentle on me. I'm old, fragile and allergic to criticism. I'm also allowed to be pissed off. I've earned (not earnt, Grrr!) the right to have a bloody good whinge.

I'd love to hear your gripes.
Email: michaelthorntonbooks@gmail.com
Be nice!

'HAITCH'

4 My grandchildren attend *government* primary schools, where to my total disdain they've been taught to say 'haitch' instead of 'aitch'. It used to be a secret Catholic thing, like the Freemasons' secret handshake! Yet, somehow, it's crept into Victoria's state school system. It's appalling, and it pisses me off. I'm seriously thinking of running for parliament so I can propose a bill to outlaw 'haitch', or, if I fail to get elected, emigrate — *NOT* immigrate!

13 LEADING PISSERS

5 Australia's *seventy* richest citizens have more wealth than the bottom *half* of the country

*

6 Australia's richest person is said to earn $33,000 *every minute*

*

7 domestic violence occurs in one in every *four* Australian homes

*

8 *forty* per cent of Australians in aged care have no visitors: no family, no friends; *no one*

*

9 eight Australians commit suicide every day — that's one loved one *every three hours*

*

10 two-thirds of Australians are overweight or obese; we're the *fattest* country in the world

*

11 one in eight Australians still smokes

*

12 each year, we give away $12 billion to charity, but we spend $14 billion on alcohol

*

13 Australian women spend $15,000 a year on make-up (when it's *character* which counts)

*

14 Australia has the costliest electricity in the world (coz our mongrel politicians sold it off)

*

15 eighty per cent of Australians gamble, wagering more per head than in any other country

*

16 *all* of the world's ten most poisonous snakes are Australian; 3,000 of us get bit annually

*

17 all up, Australians drive to *Pluto* and back twenty times each year

A RAFT OF PISSERS (1)

Here are a raft of things I wish I could ban, change, reverse, stop — or encourage/reward:

18 greed

19 chaos

20 leaf blowers

21 dopey, misguided parents who fork out $43,000 per child per year on private school fees

22 the same commercials repeated ad nauseam for products I've vowed never to buy

23 acid reflux / heartburn / indigestion — and the accompanying hiccups caused by ageing

24 when yet another pathology nurse says, with a deep sigh, 'Let's try your other arm!'

25 heavy static on the car radio just as the interesting speaker is about to make her point

26 the huge thistle which I found growing on my father's grave above his left knee

A RAFT OF PISSERS (1)

27 how my insolent children used to turn feral on me when I began to sing on road trips

28 being bucked off my horse all those years ago — and being winded something horrible

29 being bucked off my horse a second time — while still badly winded from the first fall

30 being bucked off anything — winded or not

31 how plants in Bunnings grow beautifully but when I take them home they turn to crap

32 young people on the tram with their head down, who don't stand for me

33 young people on the tram with their head up, who do stand for me (I'm not THAT old!)

34 I decided to leave some money to my school in my will

35 I decided to tell my school I was leaving some money to it in my will

36 unlike in the US, we don't have outrageously generous tax breaks for charitable giving

37 how our corrupt, mongrel bathroom scales lie to me every time I step onto them

38 people on TV shows who inadvertently let slip how long ago the episode was taped

39 the day my elder teenage son found a puddle of pus in his fried chicken

40 the time my mother nearly choked on a sausage — and my impertinent children laughed

41 guns

42 movie reviewers who are talentless and tasteless

43 how I recently found a wallet on the footpath with all manner of cards and cash inside and, after rifling through the contents, I found a name. I then located the owner on Facebook, and in a fleeting, impetuous moment of total stupidity — and out-of-character integrity — I returned said wallet to the owner, cash and all

44 wishing there was a pill for stupidity

45 climbing plants which I can never make to climb

46 fake plants which I can never make climb

47 rabid conservatives, some of whom, if you scratch real deep, have a social conscience

48 the *only* job in the world where you start at the top ... is digging a hole

49 how on earth a 3D printer can make an edible, appetising steak is totally beyond me

50 the church school which, in a huge display advertisement to attract new students, listed its major goals — but excluded *faith* (so as not to turn away agnostic prospective clientele)

51 half a large pizza is never enough

52 the total stranger who pulled up next to me in an

otherwise deserted car park, unwound his window, and whispered, *'You didn't tell anyone about this, did you?'*

53 snow skiing, which used to come naturally to me

54 water skiing, which used to come naturally to me

55 life, which used to come naturally to me

56 I sold my first house for $5,000, less than I paid for it

57 real estate agents who arrive 10 minutes late for an open inspection

58 real estate agents who don't apologise for being 10 minutes late for an open inspection

59 retail staff who hover near the front door but don't open until the *exact* opening time

60 people who confuse bought and brought

61 all four other patrons at the café are reading a 'house' newspaper, so I wait patiently for a copy to become available. A sweet old lady eventually hands me her copy, then scurries away. But, upon inspection, I discover she's pinched the puzzles section

62 AFL 'behinds' should be called 'bummers'; NRL 'conversions' should be 'got its'

63 how any living creature, which is 95% water (E Musk), can possibly have $250 billion is beyond me

64 when two ambulances with lights flashing and sirens blaring arrive at an intersection at exactly the same moment but from opposite directions, which one has right of way?

65 sad that I can't afford to buy Pumpkin Island (southern Great Barrier Reef, 15 km off the Queensland coast; the asking price being $25 million)

66 every lotto win I have is for less than $20

67 every lotto ticket I buy costs more than $20

68 why Dopey was feeling Happy; Bashful, Sleepy; Sneezy, Grumpy

69 I once asked the CEO of McDonald's, in a boardroom business briefing — and to loud gasps from around the room — how often she let her young children eat McDonald's

70 asking why I was made to castrate lambs using my teeth back when I was a jackaroo

71 asking why was I made to be a jackaroo?

72 what did they *really* get up to when Harry met Sally? (I don't think it was castration!)

73 medicines which turn my constipation into diarrhoea (which they do)

74 medicines which turn my diarrhoea into constipation (which they do)

75 hair in the basin which isn't mine

76 hair in the basin which Kass swears isn't hers, but is

77 men who shave while driving to work

78 women who shave while driving to work

79 the hospital which wrote threatening me with a thousand lashings if I am late for, or miss, an upcoming

appointment — but *didn't* give me the appointment day and time

80 not knowing how to use most of the functions on my phone

81 skin cancer-free, topless (and sometimes bottomless!) summers spent lazing on the beach

82 salami, now that it costs $28 a kilo

83 as a child, sugar-laden, chocolate marshmallow milk shakes at Hillier's after the dentist

84 my wonderful, long-gone IBM golf ball typewriter which used to write real fancy

85 my horse

86 my late sister's horse

87 my late sister

88 Peter Hudson's 727 goals for Hawthorn

89 pounds, shillings and pence — and halfpennies, threepences, sixpences and guineas

90 as a child, my precious and hugely prolific rhubarb plant

91 back in the '50s, when wool sold at auction for 'a-pound-a-pound'

92 the Beatles are over

93 dribbles on my pillow

94 the banter on radio 3AW between Ormsby Wilkins, Claudia Wright and Norman Banks

95 processing in the chapel choir while talentless scabs in the pews yelled *'Poofter'*

96 my grandparents' holiday home

97 my grandmother's Yorkshire puddings

98 Richie Benaud's cricket commentary — and wanting his take on 'Sandpapergate'

99 early that September morning in 1983 when Australia won the America's Cup

100 PM Bob Hawke on the morning we won the America's Cup saying, *'Any boss who sacks anyone for not turning up today is a bum'*

101 the thrill of watching the West Indies play cricket back when they were lethal

102 attending the Olympic Games in Melbourne in 1956, when I was six (so I was told)

103 Derryn Hinch losing his Senate seat

104 Pauline Hanson winning her Senate seat

105 I've almost forgotten what salmon tastes like

106 I well and truly *have* forgotten what lobster tastes like

107 seeing a favourite supermarket item on special the day after I bought four of them

108 finding I had *four* bolts left over after I reassembled the ride-on lawn mower

109 finding I had *five* bolts left over after I tried a second time to reassemble the ride-on

A RAFT OF PISSERS (1)

110 fishermen and fisherwomen are now called fishers; bloody ridiculous

111 he and she are now they; utter stupidity

112 the dumber the TV show, the higher its ratings (especially that 'married' show)

113 being the only dad at my daughter's grade five parent–daughter sex education evening

114 being made, along with five mothers, to assess our daughters' drawings of a penis at the grade five parent–daughter sex education evening

115 my face at the grade five parent–daughter sex education evening

116 the appalling lack of academic rigour at my agricultural college

117 graffiti and tagging (I have no idea what the difference is)

118 TV quiz show contestants who get dead easy questions wrong and hard questions right

119 how my mother never stopped reminding my sister and me she'd played at Wimbledon

120 the 'Crossing-the-Line' ceremony on the *Dominion Monarch* passenger ship, in 1955

121 being chased from the ship's swimming pool during the 'Crossing-the-Line' ceremony

122 lamb's liver when it's full of gross sinews and blood vessels

123 when the chairlift cable snapped

124 when the chairlift cable snapped with me on it

125 beaten at Scrabble by my Filipina mother-in-law, English being her *second* language

126 Paul Keating telling us it was the recession we had to have

127 finding out only after arriving at the party that it's Amway

128 awful people like me who watch car and motorbike racing for the prangs

129 people who say, *'Trust me'*

130 when my favourite pen runs out of ink, mid-se

131 seeing my togged-up, grade 6 daughter bawling her eyes out on the sidelines because the two best swimmers in her class got to swim *every* event at the inter-school meet

132 the American pastor who looked directly at me when he proclaimed from the pulpit: *'Too many of you are here on a scholarship!'*

133 churches which treat women as husband-obeying, subservient chattels

134 women who allow themselves to be treated as husband-obeying, subservient chattels

135 the guy at my local who tried to sell me a dodgy used car

136 *'anythink'* (eye witness), *'everythink'* (political

staffer), *'nothink'* (sporting commentator), *'somethink'* (talkback caller)

137 for fun, I changed my phone's ringtone to a barking dog. The next morning, at 2.30, I awoke to a nearby dog, barking loudly. I opened the window and yelled at it to desist

138 the university student sitting at the table next to us, constantly sniffing

139 gambling advertisements on TV

140 gambling advertisements anywhere

141 back when I ran a boys' school boarding house, admonishing a year 10 boy for saying *'arks'* instead of ask — only to have him tell me it was a legitimate speech impediment

142 the sadness of, and, frankly, the appalling and unacceptable road toll

143 road hoons

144 animal torture

145 people torture

146 torture of any kind

147 children dying from incurable diseases

148 adults dying from incurable diseases

149 HIV/AIDS

150 having to say sorry

151 having to hear sorry

152 horse racing

153 dog racing

154 whacko politicians with extreme agendas

155 parents *not* being charged and sentenced over their child's criminal behaviour

156 oil companies which refrain from dumping oil at sea *not* because it's illegal but because they fear getting *caught* — and admit it (like when it happened off the coast of Mexico)

157 Australia has 7,000 security firms and 150,000 security officers in an industry worth $8 billion; what does that say about us living in a well-ordered, law-abiding society?

158 opening my wallet only to find it is stone-motherless-empty

159 using the phrase peak hour 'rush' when everyone and everything is at a standstill

160 chocolate

161 six shirts which no longer fit because they've shrunk

162 my daughter's blindness at thirty-three

163 my younger son's death at twenty-eight

164 severe depression and twenty-two weeks of mental hospitalisation following my son's death

165 headaches, in particular the frequent, sharp pain I get down the left side of my head

166 male tennis players who trash our country's once impeccable sporting reputation

167 the struggle involved in trying to peel an orange just to eat the damn thing

168 overseas call centre staff who are impossible to understand

169 overseas call centre staff who I don't want to understand

170 ageing, in particular mine

171 organised religion

172 organised education

173 organised anything

174 chippies who make carpentry look easy

175 plumbers who make plumbing look easy

176 bankers who try to make outrageous corporate misbehaviour look acceptable

177 accomplished painters (of pictures, not houses, but them too, if you like)

178 meals made with sugar, salt or chilli

179 cafés which charge more than $4.50 for a large latté

180 people who say orientated when they mean oriented (ditto starting with dis-)

181 the print journalist who said *'um' sixty-four* times in a four-minute report on radio

182 stuck in a motel with only a pack of playing cards — and finding I'm one card short

183 out of Quick-Eze (first-world, old person's problem, Kass tells me)

184 promises of *'I'll get back to you'*

185 promises of *'I'm a politician and I'm here to help you'*

186 promises of *'I will love you in the morning as much as I love you tonight'*

187 promises of *'I made the online payment to your bank account this morning'*

188 the separate and, quite frankly, outrageous separate bill we get for our *hot* water

189 'diabolical' Sudoku puzzles which I cannot solve

190 'easy' cryptic crosswords which I cannot solve

191 whistle-blowers who get bullied, harassed, sacked and sued, and sometimes killed

192 dodgy builders and developers whose cost-cutting negligence taxpayers have to redress

193 selling off 'The Aussie Farm' to foreign interests — and *no one* says boo

194 good people who die too soon

195 bad people who die not soon enough

196 meanness

197 selfishness

198 hypocrisy

199 addiction

200 extravagance

201 light bulbs which are made deliberately to blow after four hours use

202 unforgiveness

203 ungraciousness

204 ingratitude

205 duplicity

206 salaries over $200,000

207 buildings taller than six storeys (ours is six storeys)

208 Christmas merchandise on sale before the first Sunday in Advent

209 Easter hot cross buns on sale before Ash Wednesday

210 anyone in power or authority with a red face who says, 'Nothing to see here'

211 people who think they are superior to me

212 people who are superior to me

213 people who leave wee on the toilet seat

214 people who leave poo in the toilet bowl

215 anyone who can afford to holiday in the Maldives

216 people who think they're the bees' knees at karaoke but in fact are tone deaf

217 people who die without a will

218 people who die with a will but without *me* in it

219 use-by dates which are unnecessary and unnecessarily alarmist

220 cricketers and cricket commentators who say *batter* instead of batsman and batswoman

221 people who think terrific means wonderful when in truth it means terrifying

222 petrol companies which make service stations lift fuel prices when it's the same petrol in their underground tank which they sold at the old price yesterday (I will never get it!)

223 women who turn angry the minute they turn thirty

224 the exorbitant cost of building major roads — $155 per *inch* per lane

225 live theatre staff who, prior to the show starting, march up and down the aisles carrying a big sign, yelling at patrons to turn off their phone — when I've already turned mine off

226 theatre goers who, just as the show starts, turn their phone back on to check Facebook

227 thugs at the football on and off the field

228 when my dentist says, 'We have two options …'

229 sycophant radio presenters who giggle in the background when the lead presenter makes a grossly inappropriate, offensive, racist, sexist or misogynist remark

A RAFT OF PISSERS (1)

230 unchristian Christians, especially those who tried hard to prevent same-sex marriage

231 people who get mentioned in the newspaper's page two gossip column

232 I never get mentioned in the newspaper's page two gossip column

233 people who begin every sentence with 'So ...'

234 'So, everyone else's dish at the restaurant always looks more appealing than mine'

235 gristle

236 lowlife who put needles in fruit to kill us

237 thunder

238 lightning

239 bushfires

240 floods

241 tsunamis

242 doctoring when it doesn't refer to medicine

243 when press freedom used to mean press freedom

244 people who blame smashed avocado for their financial ineptitude

245 boys, usually those in trouble, being called young men; boys are boys until they turn eighteen

246 how any one person can *afford* and be *allowed* to spend $84 million on electioneering

247 church leaders who say they would go to jail before reporting a confessing paedophile

248 the dog in our apartment block which begins to bark the moment daddy goes to work

249 diners at fast food outlets who are too lazy to carry their containers to the waste bin

250 imbecilic, brainless bogans on TV reality shows

251 TV reality 'builds' which reward speed over craftsmanship

252 so-called 'experts' on TV reality dating shows who promote conflict over love

253 airline passengers who applaud when the plane lands normally

254 airline passengers who stand before the seatbelt sign is switched off

255 opposition parties which poo-poo policies but do *exactly* the same when they get into power

256 when my local library doesn't have the book I ordered and which I'm impatient to read

257 the person who transfers bucket loads of beach sand onto our car's clean carpet

258 Israel and Palestine being unable, after all these *decades*, to achieve lasting peace

259 any poor dolt of an old age pensioner who still has a mortgage

260 I used 10 dollars of petrol to drive to a distant

discount warehouse sale, where I saved five dollars on product

261 any bank which needs to spend $6 million to say sorry

262 feral junior football parents

263 yet another high-profile restaurant chain is found to have underpaid its staff, by millions

264 tattoos, especially those on members of my family

265 prosperity religion: *'Please, God, make me rich, and successful, and even more rich!'*

266 how the Melbourne trams' website never has the 'Apply-Here-To-Be-A-Driver' tab active

267 using starch when I meant to use bleach

268 using bleach when I meant to use starch

269 chairs without arms and backs

270 stools — the ones you sit on, but also the other kind, if you insist

271 American Pit Bull Terriers / Dobermanns / Rottweilers / German Shepherds

272 arriving at the pub at 4 pm to find happy hour starts at 5 pm

273 arriving at the pub at 7 pm to find happy hour finished at 6 pm

274 people who never learn from their mistakes

275 fainting after stapling my thumb

276 films which I liked but to which the stupid reviewer gave only one star

277 films which I hated but to which the stupid reviewer gave five stars

278 billboards which proclaim: *'Lose weight. The aliens will eat the fat ones first'*

279 politicians who don't get it — whose only *real* policy goal is to get re-elected

280 the unfair cost of Viagra

281 the unfair cost of replacement printer ink cartridges

282 fingernails down a blackboard

283 that my car dropped $10,000 in value the minute I drove it out of the showroom

284 'shed-you-all' or 'sked-you-all?'

285 con-trib-ute or contrib-ute?

286 kill-om-etter or kilo-metre?

287 'The Chase Australia' hasn't yet thrown up a love interest for chaser Issa

288 Cadbury no longer does factory tours

289 vertically-challenged people who look at me with envy

290 slim people who look at me with pity

291 TV chefs who slice vegetables at breakneck speed without losing a finger

292 delinquent, precocious and raucous children who need a damn good thrashing

293 calling racehorses equine athletes (*WTF?*)

294 the body corporate by-law which prevents us drying our washing on the balcony

295 '*Back in the day*' when I had a decent income

296 '*She'll be right*' from the tradie hanging our new TV on the living room wall

297 the impertinence of calling customers '*walk-ins*'

298 men my age who look younger than me

299 men my age who, without success, try to look younger than me

300 café patrons who use the 'house' newspaper as a drink coaster, while I want to read it

301 my heart tells me to eat the chilli but my head tells me I'm an idiot

302 I didn't attach my bicycle to the metal pole using thick chain and heavy padlock

303 being kept waiting for 37 minutes by the locum doctor

304 the locum doctor not apologising for keeping me waiting for 37 minutes

305 the locum doctor who kept me waiting having the temerity to try not bulk billing me

306 how, if I'd been 37 minutes late for a business meeting, I'd have missed out on the deal

307 pedestrians who dawdle across intersections while on their phone

308 'what's mine is mine and what's yours is mine'

309 there is nothing more grossly stupid than Christmas-in-July

310 why do I say, repeatedly, 'Aw, yes you are ...' when I stoop to pat someone's dog?

311 a child with no life experience telling us on TV that the bank means more than money

312 discovering when I get home that one egg is broken

313 discovering when I get home that I left the chocolate bar at the checkout

314 trams no longer have a dancing, singing conductor

315 first in line but last to be called

316 I'm certain they are feeding Young Sheldon anti-growth hormones

317 people who travel overseas for a brief holiday and take half their house with them

318 traffic at a standstill on the freeway — *after* it's had four extra lanes added

319 they could never pay me enough to watch a Tom Cruise movie

320 when the child you've spent millions to raise tells you that you look old

321 when the child you've spent millions to raise doesn't pay you back

A RAFT OF PISSERS (1)

322 when the child you've spent millions to educate *begins* a sentence with 'Me and Sue...'

323 when the child you've spent millions to educate *ends* a sentence with '... to Sue and I'

324 I turned the other cheek but the same thing happened

325 vowing not to patronise criminal eateries only to find there is nowhere left to eat

326 richly-attired racegoers who worship a particular thoroughbred before it becomes glue

327 'Great Railway Journeys' I will never be able to afford

328 happy hour, when I'm on time and the cheap prices encourage me to drink beer in pints

329 our local, traditional fish-and-chip shop has suddenly gone upmarket, as have its prices

330 not a single one of the 151 members of the House of Representatives inspires me

331 not a single one of the seventy-six senators inspires me

332 Mr Ed worries me, because one should *never* bet on anything which can talk

333 non-writers who get published, especially sporting stars, who can't string together one cohesive sentence, like

334 the three biggest winners in sport are betting agencies, lawyers and surgeons

335 China

336 when we ordinary, everyday, streetwise punters are treated like complete, total mugs

337 business and charity emails which don't include the required 'Unsubscribe' facility

338 rich young people

339 rich old people

340 the insult levelled by the pharmacy when it puts my meds in a *locked box* between pick-up and payment counters — because they don't trust me not to exit without paying

341 Sunnyside nudist beach at Mt Eliza which beckons, but which I'm far too timid to visit

342 the TV reporter who asks a grieving parent, *'How does it feel ...?'*

343 advertorials

344 being let go

345 using *'at this point in time'* when it's *'at this time'* (no such thing as a point in time)

346 I've never been given my own talk show

347 failing year 11 English — twice!

348 jealous of my childhood pogo stick for being so skinny

349 using envy when jealousy is the word

A RAFT OF PISSERS (1)

350 using jealousy when envy is the word

351 no longer needing to fear premature ejaculation

352 universities which have the gall to argue for greater funding, again and again

353 university graduates driving taxis but yearning to become casino croupiers

354 silverware through an upper ear, nose, lip, forehead, belly button, genitals

355 the unbelievable, huge cost of owning a puppy

356 the brothels (as in untidiness) which were my teenage children's bedrooms

357 the other kind of brothels, about which I know absolutely nothing

358 how the recorded voice which lists the menu options gives the one I want, last

359 that our apartment balcony was built without a power point, light or tap

360 football premierships won by an interstate team

361 protesters who glue themselves to buildings, roads and handrails

362 when my paper tiger catamaran did a cartwheel — with me on it

363 reading about the *Titanic's* misfortune in my doctor's waiting room

364 when I told my GP, 'It hurts when I do this ...' and he told me not to do it

365 how new service stations always find petrol underneath

366 fast food hamburgers, which once were the size of a large bread-and-butter plate, today are little bigger than a 20 cent coin

367 the undiscussed correlation between violence on screen and violence in society at large

368 selfish pricks who dump their shopping trolley at the end of our street

369 chapped lips — and how they always happen when I don't have lip balm

370 not knowing that my car has a button to make the side mirrors turn in when I dismount

371 I too knew Banjo Paterson's full name (Andrew Barton), meaning I too could have won $1m on Millionaire Hot Seat — the only time it's been won in Australia, on 29.8.2016

372 I never score the business end of a Christmas cracker

373 bike lanes — especially ones on the driver's side of cars

374 the economic catastrophe which awaits when mortgage interest rates return to normal

375 hot air balloons which drift above our building at 6 am and make scary, firing-up noises

376 Barrie Cassidy no longer hosts ABC TV *Insiders*

A RAFT OF PISSERS (1)

377 Phil and Simon no longer have their weeknight program on 3AW

378 I've forgotten

379 bubbly, young footballer stars who have no idea what's meant by 'getting the flick'

380 not enough politicians get the flick

381 Roger Federer won't ever get the flick

382 never again will a heckler say to prime minister Menzies, 'What ya gunna do about 'ousing?' To which Menzies would reply, 'Put an "h" in front of it'

383 never again will a heckler say to prime minister Churchill, 'If I were your wife I'd feed you poison,' to which Churchill would reply, 'Madam, if I were your husband, I'd drink it'

384 to the heckler who charged Churchill with being drunk; he replied, 'And you're ugly, but I'll be sober in the morning'

385 I never got to see Don Bradman play

386 I did get to see Leigh Matthews play, but nowhere near enough

387 the TV in the doctor's waiting room is never set to ABC News 24

388 corruption

389 the KenKen puzzle in *The New York Times* is far superior to the one in *The Age*

390 getting excited about an upcoming TV show only to discover it's on pay bloody TV

391 the car salesman who saw me coming — and took a deep breath

392 enough already about Schapelle Corby

393 Gregory Peck whacking Ava Gardner with a baseball bat in *On The Beach* and my cousin James and me, aged nine, in the background in our little rubber dinghy

394 later that day Mum asked Ava Gardner what it was like to be married to Frank Sinatra

395 that no one asked this gorgeous nine-year-old movie star for his autograph

396 drought

397 dementia

398 public transport authorities which claim to meet their punctuality targets — but cheat

399 I wasn't on the No.72 tram when the fourteen-year-old stole it and drove it to Kew

400 Tom (Elliott, 3AW): *'Me and my friends used to …'* (twice in 5 mins)

401 'unseasonal climate behaviour' and 'half-pregnant'

402 when politicians talk about 'reform' they mean they're about to screw us, *again*

403 I thought of asking a friend for her gripes but then realised she'd likely steal my idea

A RAFT OF PISSERS (1)

404 I did ask the friend for her gripes, and she said, *'What a great idea for a book!'*

405 organ harvesting

406 upping the number of executions to meet higher organ harvesting quotas

407 gay conversion therapy

408 gay hate

409 any kind of conversion therapy and hate

410 talking of gay conversion and gay hate, three out of twenty-three Anglican dioceses

411 my printer won't scan

412 my scanner won't print

413 Officeworks has a smart-looking printer on sale for $55

414 Ian Henderson no longer reads the Melbourne edition of the 7 pm ABC TV News

415 my school made me repeat grade 3

416 my school realised its huge error and leap-frogged me over grade 4, to grade 5

417 having never had the foggiest as to what happens in grade 4

418 when my arm, which is poking out of the car window, won't reach the ticket machine

419 publishers' rejection emails

420 old men who go shopping in an off-white, stained singlet

421 slothfulness

422 garlic breath

423 when a football coach says to an ageing player, *'Hey, mate, we need to have a chat'*

424 Alan Joyce's salary

425 *'All the way with LBJ'*

426 how mosquitoes love me but the winning lotto numbers don't

427 overlooked by the Australian Electoral Commission to work at the last election

428 so many rural towns are dying — and no one seems to give a flying fig

429 The Harold Holt Swim Centre being named after a prime minister who drowned

430 cracked pickle forks on three Qantas 737 planes

431 the Qantas spokesman, referring to the cracked pickle forks, saying, *'She'll be right'*

432 cracked pickle forks being anything *but* right

433 Bill Bryson saying we're prosperous, well ordered, and instinctively egalitarian

434 colonoscopies

435 endoscopies

436 gastroscopies

437 the banking royal commission finds gross fraud and corruption by banks; *not possible*

438 the aged care royal commission finds gross neglect of the elderly; *can't be true*

439 the sexual abuse royal commission finds gross sexual abuse of children; *we all knew it*

440 how come ABC TV's *Escape from the City* never asks if there is Internet access?

441 embarrassing world leaders

442 incompetent world leaders

443 corrupt world leaders

444 embarrassing, incompetent and corrupt world leaders

445 leaders who screw their country's needy

446 politicians who give themselves a 10% pay rise, but offer the police just two per cent

447 politicians who don't answer the question

448 politicians who answer the question they wished they'd been asked

449 bad apples

450 bad eggs

451 baddies

452 goodies who become baddies

453 the total stranger who came up to us at our table, and said, 'Sorry I'm late'

454 the suspicious looking men at the next table, whispering, and glancing here and there

455 fishing — the world's all-time meanest joke

456 holding on to my suit just for funerals

457 the federal minister getting free family flights from a travel agency only months before the same travel agency won a $1 billion contract from the minister's department

458 'Nothing to see here,' again

459 the terrifying thought of peer pressure forcing me to climb the Sydney Harbour Bridge

460 the terrifying thought of being served tripe

461 butchers which no longer routinely stock sheep's brains

462 butchers which require me to pre-order cured beef tongue

463 cancelling my membership of the Melbourne Cricket Club — after it took seventeen years to get in, and having been a member for thirty-three years — because it's over budget

464 repeating myself

465 repeating myself

466 Boris Johnson's personal letter to me — but without the accompanying knighthood

467 how, when a celebrity or sportsperson suffers mental health issues, it makes headlines

468 drunk and dishevelled millennials in the Melbourne Cup car park — during the big race

469 TV footage of drunk and dishevelled millennials in the Melbourne Cup car park — during the big race

470 toilet paper rolls hung under, not over

471 when the SodaStream machine runs out of puff, mid-stream

472 having to check the spelling of Parramatta, Wollongong, Mooloolaba, Indooroopilly

473 being called a wanker — by a real wanker

474 slack is for cutting (or being lazy); flack is for drawing criticism

475 being a lollipop person at a school crossing is far too sweet a job

476 Niki Savva should have her own TV current affairs show

477 sales calls badgering me to sign up to the energy outfit to which I'm already signed up

478 tequila — in any form and at any time of day or night — without lemon

479 the disproportionate, high number of finance commentators with an English accent

480 the disproportionate, high number of female racing commentators with an English accent

481 litterers and loiterers, especially people who are both

482 Michelangelo didn't endow David a little more generously

483 synchronised swimming

484 red heads who get called True Blue

485 box jellyfish, coz they can kill yous

486 the Great Barrier Reef mailbox can be accessed only by ferry

487 the anti-bonking ban on federal government ministers sent bonking underground

488 no one has ever explained to me *exactly* where the 'Outback' starts or finishes

489 banking on good luck

490 good luck with banking

491 bonking, wanking bankers

492 waiters who don't know etiquette demands you serve to the left and take from the right

493 Louis Armstrong didn't live long enough to change his mind about a wonderful world

494 Pete Seeger didn't live long enough to realise we shall never overcome

495 Bob Dylan is still blowin' in the wind

496 disenchanted Canadians who wish they could secede (or at least separate) from the USA

497 I can't decide who I most envy: David Archuleta, James Blunt, Calum Scott or Ed Sheeran

A RAFT OF PISSERS (1)

498 Glenn Yarbrough didn't see the time go by

499 not that Peter Cetera knows it, but after all that we've been through

500 half of all bank robberies occur on a Friday

501 why do I fart better when I roll onto my other side?

502 will the panel on ABC TV *Insiders* ever drink the coffee?

503 sorry, but I simply cannot watch the documentary on the rescue of the twelve soccer boys and their coach from the Thai cave; I wouldn't sleep for a month after watching it

504 cave rescuers Drs Richard Harris and Craig Challen should be joint Governors-General

505 tensing, before my chiropractor cracks my back and then my neck

506 farmers who collect semen artificially, thus denying their bulls and rams having one hell of a dinky-di time

507 enough on collecting semen already

508 when Kass and I enter a near-empty restaurant and the gormless waiter asks, 'Table for two?' 'No,' I've tried replying; 'the rest of Europe will be here in a jiffy'

509 every time I board a plane — after first checking no one is watching — I make the sign of a cross on the outside of the fuselage, and I whisper, 'I'll either see Paris or Jesus!'

510 lift off

511 mid-flight (every stressful minute of it)

512 landing

513 the time I put my hand into our wood pile and saw it was two inches from a tiger snake

514 totally inadequate sentencing by courts

515 wishing people who ask to "friend" me on FB would then not try to sell me Jesus or cryptocurrency

516 the second whisky

517 the scariest word to hear from your surgeon: "*Ooops!*"

518 crocodile tours

519 people who continually whinge and whine (and who compile boring lists)

520 *'There will be no wrecking, sniping or undermining'* (ex-PM Tony Abbott)

521 my horoscope says my business acumen is second to none, which only goes to prove the stars are a total load of unmitigated, useless, crap

522 rabid greenies who sit on wooden chairs and eat and drink things that are grown

523 Christians say God gave people free will — His one *BIG* mistake

524 short-term memory loss

525 long-term memory loss

526 the incredibly perceptive gentleman in Central Park who mistook me for Sean Connery

527 sprinklers programmed to come on during the heat of the day (and burn the grass)

528 if I hear one more politician say *'hard working Australians'*

528 American men are more likely to die from breast cancer than testicular cancer

530 mould in the shower

531 when my trouser belt runs out of notches

532 frightening rises in sea levels in Micronesia and the Solomon Islands

533 instead of winners and losers — *participation awards* (really?)

534 my ridiculous and fruitless determination to persist with chopsticks

535 my once affectionate children used to call me dude; now, it's *'Hey, old man!'*

536 President Jimmy Carter's Middle East negotiator Herb Cohen saying the only negotiation he ever failed at was getting his daughter to clean her bedroom

537 Herb Cohen saying he solved the problem of his daughter's bedroom — he closed the door

538 fearing I'm about to get an ugly email from social security which will scare the bejesus out of me

539 the Parkes Elvis Festival

540 where in goodness name is Betoote?

541 please tell me what country in its right mind would stage a boat race without water?

542 'no worries'

543 'told you'

544 'fair suck of the sauce bottle'

545 I hope I die before eating meat becomes illegal

546 I hope I die before thinking sexy thoughts becomes illegal

547 I hope I die before the fond memory of having had sex becomes illegal

548 I hope I die before thinking becomes illegal

549 I hope death comes sweetly

550 who the hell dreamt up 'advertainment?'

551 'after all is said and done' is now 'at the end of the day'

552 how come we never talk about 'exit strategies' when discussing old age?

553 there is something mildly pleasing about a major horse racing fixture being rained out

554 surely *someone* knew about the wages underpayments

555 no, no, no Barnaby, never ever again

556 certain churches have so much to answer for — and so many back taxes to cough up

A RAFT OF PISSERS (1)

557 stepping onto a golf course fairway only ever to get to the trees on the other side

558 knowing that the interview I got for a job was given to me only as a courtesy

559 when I've exhausted my annual private health insurance allowance for dentistry

560 whitening toothpaste which doesn't whiten

561 trying to dig out dog poo stuck in the deep grooves on the underside of my shoe

562 when a real estate agent's drone fell on our skylight — and broke it

563 the farmer on ABC *Landline* who attached a live electric fence wire to an earthed wire

564 unbelievably dangerous, scary and chaotic road traffic in Hanoi

565 why isn't 'I Am, You Are, We Are Australian' our national anthem?

566 continuing nightmares in which I relive the sight of Jaws swallowing the bad guy

567 when I have a brain fade and realise, an *hour* later, that I've boarded the wrong tram

568 Australian pubs don't serve a Ploughman's Lunch

569 teenagers who, when you ask them a simple question, reply with 'Uh?'

570 aggressive drunks

571 aggressive non-drinkers

572 aggression

573 drunks

574 drunks who cry in my drink

575 the Bible is the most shoplifted book

576 getting a wedgie

577 real estate ads which use lots of spin but never volunteer the rates and body corporate charges

578 getting 5% off new car tyres will be of enormous help to returned soldiers battling PTSD

579 waiting for advertising agencies on Gruen's 'The Pitch' to tackle *'Privatising the ABC'*

580 the annoying woman giving directions on Google Maps must have shares in toll roads

581 negative-gearing, because I don't have it

582 franking credits, because I don't have them

583 coming second to a moron

584 lauding great athletes only to learn later that they are great drug cheats

585 when my psychologist says our time is up

586 when my podiatrist cuts a hole in my foot

587 when I cannot string out my session with my GP any longer

588 when my dentist asks the nurse for a 'block' or 'short' — yikes!

A RAFT OF PISSERS (1)

589 when Vodafone texts to say I'm out of data — and it's only the fifteenth of the month

590 when the electricity bill is imminent

591 when the car insurance and registration bills are imminent

592 when the rates bill is imminent

593 when death — and being in two minds about its merit or otherwise — looks imminent

594 when the body corporate bill arrives

595 why does life (and death) always have to be about money?

596 when unleaded petrol hits 179.9 cents per litre — just when I need to fill up

597 if SBS schedules one more documentary on Hitler...

598 being beaten by six-no-trumps

599 when I have a senior's moment and I refer to transitioning Kass as 'him,' not 'her'

600 doesn't the terribly annoying woman in the Trivago ad know it's rude to eavesdrop?

601 people say *'I'm not a hundred per cent sure'* but actually mean *'I DON'T KNOW'*

602 Michael Jackson is 'cancelled'

603 whatever it means to be 'cancelled'

604 the Queen being photographed with her hands in her pockets

605 knowing my insides don't like dairy, but having it anyway

606 corporate bonuses

607 Caroline Wilson and Corrie Perkin should be in parliament

608 I should be in parliament

609 Caroline, Corrie and I all should be in parliament — for the Common Sense Party

610 I never kept my Mickey Mouse ears

611 dumb rich people who pay for, but never use the 4-wheel drive option on their vehicle

612 ugly French men who grossly exaggerate their sexual conquests

613 dear, elderly Italian women who grossly under-exaggerate their pasta conquests

614 the Aussie dollar collapses the day before we leave on our overseas trip

615 people who drive with a child on their lap

616 people who drive with a phone to their ear

617 people who drive with a child on their lap *and* a phone to their ear

618 the constant, annoying humming noise which is our ageing fridge

619 teenage gaming millionaires

620 any kind of millionaire

621 multi-millionaires especially

623 people who can name an entire football team but not the name of the opposition leader

624 when a couple is standing together, and one says, *'my'* child instead of *'our'* child

625 John Batman chose Melbourne over Geelong as Victoria's capital because it had the MCG

626 apostrophe no-nos: we make sign's; open Sunday's; every dog has it's day; lets dance

627 when your [sic] in the airport and there's like 5,000 suitcases that look exactly like yours

628 the SBS *Mastermind* contestant who didn't know *'Green around the …'*

629 they won't ever have Judith Lucy on *The Bachelorette* because she's way too smart

630 celibacy

631 every other Friday which *isn't* pension day

632 the average Australian swallows three spiders a year

634 someone will dream up a reason to block the proposed marine wind farm off Gippsland

635 getting 'changed terms/conditions' messages, ignoring them, then waiting to be screwed

636 'Keep me in your heart'

637 'You are the reason'

638 the day I took my mother's car keys off her — after her third bingle in as many months

639 the day we moved my mother to the nursing home — after she left the gas on, again

640 late that night we went to check on Mum; she was fully dressed and waiting to go home

641 checking Facebook instead of focusing on adding to this important compilation

642 news that the Tokyo Olympics will not be broadcast on ABC radio

643 if I wasn't so busy writing this list, I'd start a crowdfunding page to raise the $1m which ABC radio says it needs to reverse its decision not to broadcast the Tokyo Olympics

644 passing on playing Santa

645 perched on a bar stool, dribbling down my singlet, reliving the good old days

646 it must be 5 pm and therefore drinks time somewhere (Ah, Gisborne, New Zealand!)

647 when the cereal box is tastier than its contents

648 the appalling and degrading insult to each and every male which is Homer Simpson

649 when there's less than one decent shot remaining in the whisky decanter

650 wearing shoes with tedious laces rather than far easier slip-ons

A RAFT OF PISSERS (1)

651 Queensland treasurer hires consultants to help her decide how to hire fewer consultants

652 things which could happen only in Queensland

653 'If you can't leave 'em, drink 'em. If you can't drink 'em, leave 'em and I'll drink 'em'

654 Mike Brady must always sing, 'Up there, Cazaly' at the Grand Final — even if it's a video

655 being told there is still time

656 being told to bide my time

657 being told my time is up

658 waiting for Christmas

659 waiting for Godot

660 how many consecutive ads are allowed in one TV commercial bracket? Is fifteen okay?

661 Hawthorn for premiers in 2030

662 taking AFL to China is a total waste of time, because they'd re-educate it

663 four-year-olds playing the three wise men. First wise man says to baby Jesus: 'I bring you gold.' Second wise man: 'I bring you myrrh.' Third wise man: 'Frank sent this!'

664 I so miss trekking the Spanish Camino de Santiago de Compostela, stopping one night at an albergue (dormitory) and hearing a beautiful voice (on CD) of the incomparable Canadian singer Loreena McKennitt singing 'Greensleeves'

665 people who steal other people's ideas; as a boy in the '60s, I had a brilliant idea about inventing a portable, cordless device which back then I tentatively called a ... 'mobile phone'

666 president of IBM saying (in 1943) there'd be a world market for maybe *five* computers

667 president of 20th Century Fox saying (in 1946) people soon would tire of staring at a plywood box every night

668 president of a vacuum company saying (in 1955) nuclear-powered vacuum cleaners would probably be a reality within 10 years

669 founder of a tech company saying (in 1995) the Internet would catastrophically crash within the year

670 Microsoft executive saying (in 1997) that Apple was as good as dead

671 when my car won't fit in a vacant space because a bogan has parked across two spaces

672 peak sporting bodies which make such appalling decisions, and so often

673 so wish I could hear Scotty McCreery sing 'The First Noel' — live

674 so wish I could hear Nathan Pacheco and David Archuleta sing 'The Prayer' — live

675 so wish I could see Loreena McKennitt sing

A RAFT OF PISSERS (1)

'Greensleeves' and 'Penelope's Song' — live (Penelope was my sister)

676 so wish I could meet Jesus — live (yes, I'm prepared to be severely reprimanded)

677 what was *Game of Thrones* about, anyway?

678 so wish they'd make another series of *Downton Abbey* before Maggie Smith carks it

679 bring back *Upstairs, Downstairs*

680 they can put a man on the moon but they can't organise online voting

681 Oscar Wilde was right: *'Forgive your enemies because nothing will piss them off more'*

682 Norman Crosby was correct when he said, *'When you go to court you are putting your fate in the hands of twelve people who aren't smart enough to get out of jury duty'*

683 Clarence Darrow was correct to say: *'When I was a boy, I was told anybody could become president; now I'm starting to believe it'* (never more true than in 2016)

684 the KFC outlet in Alice Springs applied for a Michelin star

685 when my blind daughter criticises my driving

686 Australia has the highest incidence of skin cancer in the world

687 someone told me Bushells is better

688 someone told me Dilmah is better

689 someone told me Lipton is better

690 someone told me Tetley is better

691 someone told me Twinings is better

692 someone told me coffee is best

693 people who answer a question with a question — who wants to know?

694 when the surgeon calls in sick

695 that section of the windscreen which the wipers never get

696 people who don't use their indicator

697 people who use their indictor *after* they've moved into my lane

698 people who drive alone in the transit lane, which is set aside for two-person vehicles

699 drivers who don't get caught and fined for driving alone in a two-person transit lane

700 the only drop of rain which falls from the sky is the one which lands on my head

701 car sticker: 'I got laid at the Hamilton B&S' (Bachelors & Spinsters Ball)

702 another person has unfriended me

703 when I have more lids than bowls

704 shoppers who rifle through their handbag for money only *after* they're told the cost

705 our highly-priced vacuum cleaner doesn't pick up Kass's hair

706 never trust a five-year-old

707 five-year-old to CEO at company annual family picnic: *'My dad says you're an arsehole'*

708 five-year-old: *'Look, mum; that policeman has handcuffs like the ones in your bedroom'*

709 five-year-old, when the priest stood again to speak at the baptism: *'Oh, no; not him again'*

710 five-year-old asked at Sunday School what he'd do if he found money: *'Finders, keepers'*

711 five-year-old, while waiting in line with his mother at the deli, folds their ticket number in half, stuffs it into her cleavage, and says, *'Go get yourself something nice'*

712 I forgot to charge (both my phone and for my time)

713 there will never be another ewe

714 there will never be another *Mrs Doubtfire*

715 falling asleep during *Phantom of the Opera*

716 opinion polls finally have proved that people lie to pollsters

717 missing Jon Faine, but enjoying Virginia Trioli

718 radio hosts who say *'The minister will be talking to you ...'* when it's *'... to me'*

719 spilling peas on the floor

720 spilling more peas on the floor

721 damn it, spilling even more peas on the floor

722 governments which have loads of money to splash at elections but not at other times

723 three into ten doesn't

724 neither does six into twenty

725 bothering to argue with a call centre person

726 bothering to argue with someone online

727 bothering to argue with someone from the government

728 bothering to argue with someone at home

729 people who don't reciprocate with a return dinner invitation

730 people who don't go home immediately after they've eaten the meal we've provided

731 desperately wanting to go to bed — alone

732 so-called friends who don't send a thank you note (or an email, at least) after a dinner

733 costly plant food which hasn't made a skerrick of difference to our balcony plants

734 my father's alcoholism

735 my father falling to his death over a St Kilda Hotel balcony when I was thirteen

736 learning the hard way what's meant by a pub crawl

737 throwing up and then crawling over it while on a pub crawl

738 high up a tree and avoiding cutting my leg off with my chainsaw thanks only to luck

739 venturing out to buy a new $1200 chainsaw but returning instead with a $1200 painting

740 so-called friends who cut off all contact after you divorce their friend

741 so-called friends who cut off all contact after you come out

742 so-called friends who cut off all contact after you divorce their friend *and* come out

743 dutifully checking the death notices each morning to make sure I'm not included

744 the clergyman who told his footballer son at half time, *'Number 28 has to go!'* To which the son replied, *'But dad, I'll get rubbed out and lose two match payments.'* To which his padre father said, *'I'll make up the payments!'*

745 hollow promises that whipping racehorses one day will be a thing of the past

746 sometimes, when I'm alone, I cry

747 saying to a waiter, *'I'll grab a flat white'* instead of, *'Please may I have a flat white'*

748 people, especially millennials, who end conversations with the dreaded 'Cheers'

749 people, especially millennials, who say 'like' as in *'I'm like going to like visit the pub'*

750 corporates pumping millions into sporting sponsorship

751 *my* superannuation fund pumping *my* millions into sporting sponsorship

752 recalling the time when one was young, handsome and comfortable

753 Canadian children's television host Art Linkletter complaining that his wheat crop in Western Australia didn't grow ... because they sowed the seeds upside down

754 Linkletter later being offered more (albeit barren) farming land on Western Australia's north-west coast, and declaring, *'Beachfront in California costs $1,000 per square foot; at five cents a square mile it has to be a bargain. I'll take it!'*

755 gullible (but still funny) Canadian children's television hosts

756 I forgot my password (all twelve of them)

757 I forgot my Medicare number

758 telling a young couple that sex before marriage will send them blind (something like that)

759 *not* telling a young couple that *not* having sex before marriage could lead to problems

760 dreading the fate of the horse which came last (the animal sustained a shattered pelvis)

A RAFT OF PISSERS (1)

761 were it not for the '7.30' television exposé, what would have happened to that horse?

762 the only difference between co-joined private and public hospitals is carpet on the floor

763 politicians who have an epiphany

764 wishing more politicians would have an epiphany

765 obscenely wealthy people showing off their obscene wealth

766 private schools getting public money to buy million-dollar properties around them

767 public schools making do with portable classrooms without cooling, heating or water

768 war crimes

769 telling an apprentice to fetch a left-handed screwdriver

770 telling an apprentice to fetch a short time

771 coral reef bleaching

772 charities which are so grateful for your donation, they send a request for another one with the receipt for your first gift

773 telemarketers who hear me weep on the phone and promise unequivocally to take me off their database

774 being called again the following night by the *same* lying telemarketing outfit

775 North Sydney mayor saying the local swimming pool is in *regional* Australia

776 debating that black is white

777 religious fanatics who pray the 2017 same-sex marriage legislation can be overturned

778 wondering if Todd Sampson wears a collar-and-tie to Qantas board meetings

779 I didn't know mines and power stations don't pay rates

780 I *did* know private schools and universities don't pay rates

781 Melbourne's Boroondara municipality has sixty-nine properties owned by private schools which, combined, avoid $1.4 million in rates; one principal said his school *should* pay rates

782 that major media is running full-page ads calling out government secrecy, is alarming

783 I'm not perfect and I don't have *all* of the answers, just most of them

784 I can't say a single bad thing about Ashleigh Barty because she is such a superb role model for every girl and boy — so good, and so wonderfully well brought up

785 politicians who sniff the wind, and when an issue has 51% support, running with it

786 how can a Leunig cartoon, which depicts a mother so preoccupied with Instagram that she doesn't notice her baby has fallen out of its pram, generate so much outrage?

787 the all-woman panel on Q&A promulgating rabid man-hate — an absolute disgrace

788 activist now means terrorist; lobbyist means dignitary; retired means sponger

789 an update please on how much the Sri Lankan family on Christmas Island has cost us

790 having a messy garden is now called 'rewilding' (truly?)

791 truffles — totally overrated crap

792 with so much community angst about, I no longer feel alone

793 I used to say that so many things were better than sex; these days, I'm not so sure

794 right-leaning people who become lefties

795 lefties who become right-leaning

796 fence-sitters

797 Brexiteers

798 Trumpeteers

799 calls for New Zealand to become Australia's seventh state — with Jacinda as PM

800 how today, on the same page, *The Age* ran two sentences ending with a preposition

801 explaining to a teenager who Graham Kennedy was

802 explaining to a teenager what a shower and a haircut are

803 explaining to a teenager what a pen, letter, envelope and stamp are

804 explaining to a teenager what a cheque book and the concept of saving are

805 explaining to a teenager what an answering machine was

806 explaining to a teenager what sitting at the dining table for dinner used to be about

807 Buddy Franklin moving to Sydney; Cyril Rioli returning to Tiwi Islands

808 why does Kass keep calling me *'Baby'* when I'm seventy-one, already?

809 The preacher who began his sermon: *'The pizza you had last night was not awesome; Jesus is awesome!'*

810 bouncy salespeople, when I'm totally not in the mood

811 taxi drivers, who don't pull right over when picking-up or dropping-off

812 when Filipinos say *'fall in line,'* they mean *'please queue here'*

813 being asked by eleven-year-old on the drive to school, *'Dad, what's a condom?'*

814 replying to eleven-year-old, *'I'm not sure; ask your mother when you get home'*

815 when, 30 minutes after an arthroscopy, a nurse says,

'The physio will be here any moment' (and me replying, 'But I won't')

816 scuff marks on my feelings

817 scuff marks on my pride

818 scuff marks on my tolerance

819 scuff marks on my precious reindeer jacket

820 11,000 scientists from 153 countries concluding, 'We declare clearly and unequivocally that planet Earth is facing a climate emergency'

821 even if the above were only partly true (and IT IS FULLY TRUE), shouldn't we be doing everything in our God-given power to save the planet for our great-grandchildren?

... and ACCEPT the science!

822 the nasty person who just unfriended me clearly didn't like my climate science views

823 wanting my ego stroked

824 being told to chill

825 Kass telling me that mine is a first-world, white-person's problem

826 threatening to send Kass back to the Philippines where she belongs

827 when I didn't know that the 'LOL' which I got from my boss didn't mean *Lots of Love*

828 total chaos at airports worldwide since cheap travel became affordable for the masses

829 the ridiculous, high cost of long-haul rail travel in Australia

830 vomiting when I'm unwell; spewing when I'm pissed off

831 people who are single and call themselves 'self-partnered' (you're joking!)

832 being told by the government (proudly) that our gross national debt is $546 billion

833 why doesn't the government just print $546 billion — and pay it back to whomever?

834 being told the annual interest 'payment' on our gross national debt is $18.2 billion

835 not knowing to whom I should send the $18.2 billion interest, even if I could

836 why does the government tell me about all of this debt and interest? (What does it expect me to do: forego my old age pension so the debt can be retired, like me?)

837 stressing over buying, bringing home and installing a new printer

838 like everything else in life which initially causes me to stress out, successfully bringing home and installing the said printer — and then wondering what all the fuss had been about

839 stress from filling out government forms — and later wondering what the fuss was about

840 stress over whether I can move my bowels — and later wondering why all the fuss?

841 stress over getting to the doctor on time — then being made to wait for 30 minutes

842 stress over making ends meet — then winning $18.65 from a $25 lotto ticket

843 stress over whether I would wake up today (bummer — I did)

844 bogans who hold their knife and fork pointing in the air above their dinner plate

845 bogans who chew with their mouth open

846 bogan guests who fart at the dinner table, and then offer a pathetic, *'I had to'*

847 bogans who use their dessert spoon as the soup spoon

848 preferring an innie over an outie

849 the guest at the dinner party (there's always one) who is horribly argumentative

850 the guest at the dinner party (there's always one) who becomes aggressively drunk

851 *'cya'*

852 *'hey, yous'*

853 *'bogged, broke, buggered!'* (college student's telegram to principal, sent from Fink)

854 the older I get, the more agreeable I become to Australia's Defence budget

855 the older I get, the more fearful I am that I keep waking up each morning

856 the older I get, the more I worry about the aged care *industry* — and being put there!

857 the older I get, the more complaining and intolerant I find myself becoming

858 how, when President Obama gave all that money to Wall Street to help struggling punters get through the GFC, the mongrel bankers went and split the whole damn lot among themselves as *extra bonuses*

859 when it rains on my parade

860 when a fox broke in and eight [sic] our ate [sic] chooks (sick)

861 sportsmen and women falling to their knees and crying when they lose

862 hearing a snow boarder bear down on me

863 how for my acute indigestion my GP prescribed Coca-Cola — to burn off the blockage

864 government monopolies

865 government-controlled corporate monopolies

866 I say we (re-)nationalise all of the power companies — and make me boss of them

867 I say we privatise parliament — or maybe it already has been without us knowing

868 squeegee marks on the windows after I've struggled to put back the fly screens

869 texting a smiley face instead of actually saying *'I'm truly sorry, darling; forgive me'*

870 I've not been invited to the MCC Committee Room for drinks

871 overlooked to be Tony Jones's successor as host of Q&A

872 overlooked to be the summer stand-in for Neil Mitchell

873 waiting to be asked to fill in, as and when required, for Virginia Trioli

874 footballers not knowing the National Anthem so instead they mouth 'Three Blind Mice'

875 logging

876 cutting down trees

877 logging and cutting down trees

878 the way poor Adam fell for the old 'one-bite-of-the-apple' trick

879 miners given unlimited amounts of precious water ahead of struggling Aussie farmers

880 chasing but never catching the impossible dream

881 the lengths to which some people go to chase the impossible dream

882 the entitlement of having separate 'his and her' matching bathroom basins

883 advocating never to pay a ransom demand except when it's your child who's taken

884 I thought betting ads weren't allowed until after 9 pm (it should be thus)

885 the appalling mis-treatment perpetrated on young people on the autism spectrum

886 the economy is slow; I know, let's build another gigantic sporting stadium

887 'Introduce him to a good girl and he'll get over it' (parishioner, about a gay teen)

888 members running out of the House of Reps to avoid the same-sex marriage vote

889 I managed to walk only 543 km of the 800 km Camino de Santiago de Compostela

890 seeing Rod McEwen sing at B. B. King's Club & Grill in New York City

891 a positive email from Rod McEwen allowing me to quote his lyrics

892 sadly missing Rod McEwen — his music, his voice and his wonderful poetry

893 bogans who have no idea who Rod McEwen was

894 on TV, a graphic cup full of disgusting, oozing, grey tar, equal to what's inside a smoker's lungs, yet still not graphic or scary enough to make people *STOP SMOKING*

895 Scotch-and-Passiona never caught on

896 there is something mildly weird about a badly injured, returned soldier getting a penis and scrotum transplant — and everything — and I mean *everything* — working properly again

897 living next door to a teenage drummer

898 'Living Next Door To Alice'

899 who the f*** is Alice?

900 first it was cracked pickle forks on shonky planes, next it's diesel particulate filters!

901 Peter FitzSimons's excellent Andrew Ollie Media Lecture wasn't long enough

902 the pre-match musical entertainment at the AFL Grand Final was far too long

903 the pre-race musical entertainment at the Melbourne Cup was far too short

904 parents who think their smelly, precocious, snotty-nosed, belligerent brat is special

905 people in the wealthiest suburbs give the least to the telethon

906 failing to get the nine-letter word — and then, suddenly, it springs from Kass's lips

907 the maintenance guy at work who'd get the nine-letter word looking over my shoulder

908 forced to sit in the middle of a five-seat row unless I pay extra, which I refuse to do

909 still feeling guilty for having once flown business class

910 'Sale Must End Monday' — a total, unmitigated lie

911 'any 6 donuts for $15'; 1kg of sugar for $2

912 the Queensland MP who bought a posh Mercedes for his new, young bride. Trouble is, it got delivered to the ex-wife, who seized the moment, sold the car and pocketed the cash

913 'Just call me angel of the morning, angel'

914 bagpipes — unless they are playing 'Highland Cathedral' or 'You're the Voice'

915 the sportsman's father who said only those baptised by him will be 'saved'

916 intolerance towards indifference

917 indifference towards intolerance

918 persecution of LGBTIQ — yet *WE WON* the postal vote *AND THE LEGISLATION*

919 churches which allow women to preach, but which the Bible says is a big no-no

920 churches which allow clergy to marry, but which Catholics believe is unbiblical

921 taking the Bible and many of its outdated rules-for-life literally, without considering how times in which we now live have changed (e.g. we no longer write on slate)

922 biblical, unbiblical, monosyllable, drivel, whatever

923 discrimination

924 inconsistency

925 selectivity

926 four clergy, during a tea break at an inter-faith

conference, discuss the start of life. The Catholic priest says life begins at conception, no question. The Uniting Church minister says the fetus needs to be partially developed. The Anglican minister says it's for people to make up their own mind. Then the rabbi speaks up: *'You guys have got it all wrong; life begins when the kids leave home and the dog dies'*

927 the church minister who said he joined the priesthood because it was the closest thing to acting, that paid

928 defendant asks judge if he might be excused *'because my wife is due to conceive.'* The man's lawyer jumps to his feet, *'Err, Your Honour, I think my client means his wife is about to deliver.'* The judge responds, *'Either way, I think we should let him be there!'*

929 people who can solve a Rubik's Cube

930 *'Somewhere in my youth or childhood, I must have done something good'*

931 The day our gorgeous grey Fergie tractor became intractable

932 university English professor said on radio 'going forward' twice in two minutes

933 when you so wish you could undo or reverse something you've done or said, but can't

934 losing valuable, irreplaceable breeding stock during a severe drought

935 unbearable, tantrum-throwing brattish children on cruise ships (should be in school)

936 having to walk past — and be tempted by — banks of poker machines in order to get from one end of the cruise ship to the other

937 having to weave one's way through — and be tempted by — the never-ending array of duty-free goods (especially cheapish Scotch) in order to get to the airport departure gate

938 finding one's departure gate has been changed, having to walk back through duty free

939 five thousand Australians turn eighty each week

940 being late for something important

941 being early for something unimportant

942 father to son: 'I'll show you how to make a model plane if you show me how to pick a lock'

943 I'm happy to have an Australia (ID) Card because I've nothing to hide

944 I'm going to regret saying this

945 I wasn't given even the smallest say in the tiny matter of circumcision

946 I told you I'd regret it

947 subordinates who stand behind their political leader (who's on-camera), nodding at his boss's huge weeping zit

948 backing my brand-new car into a Stobie pole (South

Australian power pole) — and the subsequent teasing from three brattish, ill-mannered and over-indulged children

949 tedious radio and television commercials which lack even a smidgeon of creativity

950 I've never been hired to write a radio or television commercial, which is a skill I firmly believe I possess

951 being the nominated driver when I didn't want to be, because *I wanted to drink*

952 good and sincere people who try hard, yet fail

953 wankers who don't try at all, yet still manage to succeed

954 actors make good politicians, but politicians never make good actors

955 The American War (as the Vietnamese call it)

956 President Johnson's lies about the Gulf of Tonkin 'incidents,' which he used falsely and dishonestly to justify starting the war in Vietnam

957 the enormous losses suffered in Vietnam by all sides

958 the appalling treatment of heroic Australian soldiers upon their return from Vietnam

959 today's Vietnam so warmly welcomes western visitors

960 there is a boarding school in Queensland which takes children from grade two

961 needing to keep a baseball bat beside the bed to repel teenage home invaders

962 bogans who sport a grinning disposition and a baseball cap

963 smugness and a baseball cap

964 I've been developing a family board game called 'Abuse, Corruption and Neglect in Australia' — but there isn't enough room on the board

965 budgie smugglers — and politicians who wear them

966 I've given loads more flowers than I've received

967 I love receiving flowers

968 everyone is going through something we can't see

969 anxiety tablets dispensed by the nurse according to 'PRN' ('Please Right Now')

970 Richard Carlton can never again ask Bob Hawke what it's like to have blood on his hands

971 of course the mothers will go to the weddings; otherwise they won't get their faces on the telly

972 capers in pasta

973 cloves in apple strudel

974 jalapenos in a Subway

975 I read some of these amazingly pithy pieces to Kass, and she said, 'Booooooring!'

976 who on earth could possibly fill David Attenborough's shoes?

977 why didn't all three European judges on *The Voice, Italy* 'turn' for Leo Ristorto?

978 the TV personality who returned from maternity leave only to be sacked because she no longer could squeeze into her size 10 dress

979 opening the paper to find the show into which an up-and-coming writer has put her heart and soul received only one star — from a reviewer without a creative bone in its body

980 'Sex in the City'

981 sex in the country

982 sex

983 Sydney people say 'sic-ard-er'; Melbourne folk say 'sic-aid-er'

984 Sydney people say 'be-cors'; Melbourne folk say 'be-coz'

985 struggling to remember *The Joy of Sex*

986 after you retire, the only difference between Friday and Saturday is the thickness of the newspaper

987 being too lazy — and too scared — to make an appointment to see my cardiologist

988 making poor decisions

989 thinking back to my 2004 quadruple heart bypass — and starting to get fidgety

990 mechanic says to cardiologist, 'How come I can give your car engine a complete rebuild, yet you charge fifty times more to fix my heart?' The cardiologist replies, 'Ever tried to do the engine rebuild with the motor still running?'

991 at the previous election no Liberal wanted to know Jim Molan

992 oh, how I wish a radio presenter would stop an interviewee mid-sentence, and say, 'Could you please not start every sentence with "so" — and for God's sake stop saying "um"'

993 political strategists who argue the party must play on people's fears, not on positive issues

994 finding time to drive to namesake Thornton to have a picnic by the Rubicon River

995 I seriously want to know why my children are more handsome than their father

996 I seriously want to know why my children are not as stupid as their father

997 Australia has six times more sheep than people (why I mention this I have no idea)

998 'Everybody hurts, sometimes'

999 law professor says *very unique.* Can't be. It's either unique, or it's not; idiot!

1000 memo to Julia Zemiro: I'm available any time to be your subject on 'Home Delivery'

1001 in the Four Corners episode on literacy, the reporter said to camera: *'the students that ...'*

1002 and from a teacher on the same program: 'this student has had opportunities given to them'

1003 the White Lady looks like she's seen a ghost

1004 beetroot stains on my bib

1005 spilled milk on the car seat

1006 personal name badges with writing in a fancy font but far too tiny to read

1007 mirrors which make me look like a pregnant giraffe

1008 WA Greens senator Jordon Steele-John (youngest federal MP)

1009 looking everywhere for the top of my pen — finally finding it between my lips

1010 stupid is as stupid does

1011 does artificial intelligence mean having a plastic brain?

1012 never once used our dishwasher — but it looks cool

1013 this book is sophisticated because only sophisticated people are likely to read it

BROTHERLY LOVE

1014 How would you be? You take a package on an overseas flight for your *brother*. Trouble is, in the bag he said to put in the overhead bin is a bomb hidden inside a meat grinder.

FINANCIAL WOES

It pisses me off that I'm so hopeless with money. Always have been. Here's why:

1015 I didn't have a father to teach me about money

1016 my mother knew zilch about money

1017 being at boarding school, I didn't have a paper round to learn to value of money

1018 even if I did have a paper round, I would have spent the money on something silly

1019 at nineteen, I got my first loan — for a car! (interest rate of 28%); apparently 28% is a lot

1020 at twenty-six, I borrowed again — for a house (interest, 18%); apparently 18% is still a lot

1021 what I earned from writing for a newspaper while at agricultural college, I didn't save

1022 that I chose agriculture — with limited value — when I should have studied criminology

1023 in my twenties, I did a lot of snow skiing, which cost a fortune

1024 I've had three marriages when one would have been sufficient (don't ask which one)

1025 I had three children when one would have been sufficient (don't ask which one)

1026 I put said children through private schools, when state schools would have done fine

1027 I've had thirteen houses, twelve cars and four dogs

1028 I bought a billiard table instead of putting a deposit on an extra block of land

1029 I bought a houseboat, the 'boat' bit standing for 'Bring Out Another Thousand'

1030 I bought a yacht — akin to standing under a shower tearing up hundred-dollar notes

1031 I've bought far too many (non-winning) lotto tickets

1032 my superannuation balance is well below the 'Ask Noel' column average in *The Age*

1033 I eat salami

1034 I drink whisky

1035 I buy lunch at Subway, when a salad roll prepared at home would cost two-thirds less

1036 I buy birthday and Christmas presents for four grandchildren; gifts they don't need

1037 I have my car cleaned by a bunch of young guys for $39 instead of washing it myself

1038 I put money in the church plate (with *no* guarantee of a return on investment)

1039 I have the occasional flutter on poker machines

1040 I've bought four engagement rings (current spouse sent her first one down the sink)

1041 I push the full-flush button when a half-flush would do fine

1042 I keep meaning to install a three-minute timer with a loud siren in the shower (for her!)

1043 in winter, we use the air-conditioner to heat the apartment, when we should just freeze

1044 in summer, we use the air-conditioner to cool the apartment, when we should just fry

1045 I recorded a CD of my favourite eighteen songs — exquisite voice, but costly as all get up

1046 I've never robbed a bank, knowingly cheated at a supermarket self-checkout, or *taken* money *from* the church plate

1047 I keep participating (and every time, lose) in Melbourne Cup sweeps, and raffles

1048 we've been on three (albeit budget-priced) Pacific cruises

1049 we use top quality plastic food wrap when we should make do with the cheap crap

1050 I once flew business class and got a cheap, tiny, plastic model plane for my $3,900

1051 too often, I leave the water running while I brush my teeth

1052 I don't tell lies to regulators

1053 sometimes, I'm a touch loose with the truth

1054 I love smashed avocado, oysters, salmon and Johnnie Walker

1055 I've not worked for a bank, learned to cheat, become CEO and trouser $14m a year

1056 Michael and frugality are mutually exclusive concepts

1057 I've never bothered to seek professional financial counselling (only psychiatry!)

1058 I've not written a bestseller — until now

MILLENNIALS

1059 Developers no longer put kitchens in new apartments because millennials don't cook!

SUPERMARKETS (1)

1060 Our biggest supermarket, Australia's largest employer, announces how over nine years it underpaid 5,700 staff by an estimated $300 million. Didn't *anyone* do their sums?

*

1061 *'Two for ...'* price tags. I don't want TWO. I want ONE. One block of chocolate is enough to bring on diabetes. Why would I want to get it sooner? At the accompanying bottle shop, I want twenty-four cans (one slab), not forty-eight cans. Goodness knows my liver is past its use-by date.

*

1062 Items on 'special' shout out the price on big, bright yellow labels. Items subjected to a recent price hike carry a tiny label with the price in small black type. Are we *this* gullible?

SUPERMARKETS (1)

1063 Things come on as special in the week that neither my pension nor I can afford them!

1064 Having to traipse to the rear of the store for milk is an insult to my intelligence and legs.

1065 Register 4 opens as finally, finally, finally, I get to the front of the queue at register 3.

1066 The university student at the self-serve checkout next to me scanned mushrooms ($12/kg) as bananas ($3/kg). I watched him. And *I* got threatened with life imprisonment for genuinely forgetting (remember, I'm now seventy-one) to scan the 15-cent plastic bloody bag.

1067 The checkout child asks how I am, but when I say, 'I've been diagnosed with an extended bowel,' she clams up. The poor things aren't taught to converse or empathise.

1068 I missed qualifying for the discount fuel coupon because I spent only $29.99.

DRIVING (1)

1069 *Every* traffic light I come to, turns red when I'm exactly 73.5 metres back from it.

*

1070 To repel tailgaters, I'm installing in my boot a large neon sign which, with the push of a button on the dashboard, rises, and in big red letters, flashes, 'BACK OFF ARSEHOLE.'

*

1071 Why would someone buy the Rolls-Royce from the showroom down the road from us when the same amount of dosh could *build and equip TEN, full, K-Yr12 schools* in Africa?

*

1072 If the sign protruding from the boot (see above) doesn't stop tailgaters, Plan B sees a spray gun rise and shoot 10 litres of blood-red paint over the offending vehicle's bonnet.

*

1073 When I went for my driver's licence (in a taxi!) at a country police station in 1967, I recall every road rule ended with ... '... *when safe to do so.*' Today, cars burst out of side streets into my line of traffic, just metres ahead of me, causing me to brake hard. I'm sure all of today's road rules end with '... *IF YOU CAN GET AWAY WITH IT.*'

*

1074 To get to our home we use a narrow street, which requires one car to pull over to allow the other car to pass. Good manners demand the driver of the unhindered car give a courtesy wave to the driver who's pulled over. God save the bogan Range Rover driver who was too damn selfish, too bereft of manners and too ugly to give me the courtesy wave.

*

1075 If Plans A and B (see above) don't work and the tailgater pursues and kills me, I want my epitaph to read, 'He did his bit for road safety.'

DATING

Between marriages, I used a dating agency to try to find love. I shouldn't have.

1076 The agency promised eight *'perfect matches'* — for $2,000. Mustering all of my limited courage, and casting aside huge fears of rejection, I signed the agency's agreement and paid up, hand on heart! It wasn't long before I wished I could have rewritten the firm's initial questionnaire, the one given to female clients. I would restart the survey with a new first question: *'Is your primary motivation in using our service to find a sugar daddy?'* The first *three* women with whom I was matched were midlife-crisis girls from Brighton; they all wanted to continue the tennis playing lifestyle to which they were accustomed — the one they had before their rich husband ditched them for a younger model. The fourth date was with an AFL footballer's 'ex'. She was 4'6" to my 6'4." (How did this small detail escape the agency?) From the moment we sat down at the Indian restaurant, silence reigned. She looked everywhere — but at me! After thirty of the most awkward and wasted minutes of my life, I excused myself and went to the bathroom. There, I took a fifty dollar note from my wallet, returned to the table, and slid the cash under her plate. I then ran to my car. Prospect No.5 asked to meet at a city hotel, where in anticipation she'd booked a room! I met prospect No.6 at a café, but we agreed before the coffee came that it was pointless. Candidate No.7 was another tennis player; she even wore her tennis outfit to our coffee date! Meeting No.8 was a pleasant enough woman, and while I think life with her could have worked, nothing came of it. That was that! The whole exercise was a complete waste of time. I resumed the solitary life to which I'd become accustomed, conscious I'd wasted two thousand precious dollars — and done irreparable damage to my self-esteem. Not to mention the good money wasted on the vasectomy!

LETTER TO BUS COMPANY

1077 'Dear HR person (I-know-your-name-but-I-don't-want-to-give-you-oxygen), I wanted you to know that I'm almost over that you didn't hire me to drive one of your ageing buses. It was going to be a job where, as a proud senior citizen, I could have given back meaningfully to society, as well as pay my ever-increasing household bills. I did, however, wish to point out what you missed out on. I'm actually quite a smart cookie, equal I'm sure to any of your other drivers. I finished your written exam in what the supervisor said was record time. He seemed shocked at how quickly I put down (then pocketed) the pen. Was I too clever for yous? Five-times-six equals 43, right? Bradman played squash! During the driving test, I didn't mean to run the red light, or skittle that pedestrian. Shit just happens. And you didn't need to apologise as you showed me out the door; apologise that your smart-arse colleague on the interview panel had dared to ask me how I'd handle young feral bogans when they screamed abuse at me, which he said they surely would do. Okay, so saying I would carry a ten-inch *blade might not have been prudent, but he did put me on the spot. And in answer to your questions as to whether I'd be willing to work end-to-end twelve-hour shifts, or do one-hour stints with an unpaid, six-hour break drinking your appalling instant coffee in the staff room, I said yes. I lied. I'd prefer not to go home at all. Was it because I said my career goal was to become CEO of your company that my fate was sealed? Or was it because not long ago I lost six demerit points, was fined $580 and had my licence confiscated for six months after I exceeded a country speed limit by 43 km/hr? Who cares if I were to crash a few buses? I saw you have lots of them out in the yard. Do you want to know the real reason I was pissed off by my failure to win you over, Ms? It is this: I always thank the driver as I get off one of your buses and, as a driver myself, I was hoping I would get my ego similarly stroked. You see, I thrive on praise. No hard feelings, Ms. I'm thinking of becoming an Uber driver. Have a good day. All the best, Michael'*

RANDOM PISSERS

1078 'Reverse mortgaging' and other equity-freeing financial cons. Here we have spin-advertisers spruiking in silky tones how we elderly can borrow against the value of our home, saying it's the best idea since bottled whisky. Signing away the equity in our home is crazy. The upbeat voice on the radio and TV makes it sound like a gift from heaven. But, if we take it up, we die broke. And in the meantime, we worry, endlessly. Signing away our home equity is the last thing we fragile, easily-stressed old folk should do.

*

1079 An email pops up saying I've won a car. I scroll down and it says, *'Click here to go into the draw to win a car!'* False, misleading, total sham. The fraud squad should be called.

*

1080 I've successfully nominated three people for an Australia Day or Queen's Birthday Honour, but no one has ever nominated me. How unfair is that!

*

1081 Fifty-eight years ago, but still clear in my mind, my boarding school housemaster told thirteen-year-old me to take off my jacket, and bend over the edge of his desk. Flexing his metre-long bamboo cane, he declared, *'This is going to hurt me a lot more than it will you!'*

*

1082 *Three* out of *five* over-50s who receive the free, bowel cancer test kit *toss it out!*

*

1083 I'm the first car at a red light and looking forward to a quick getaway. A motorcyclist squeezes past and parks dead in front of me, my chance of getting away first blown to smithereens. The lights turn green. And the motorbike stalls!

*

1084 A sticker on the car in front says, *'Honk if you love Jesus. If you don't, call 0417... ...*

SEXISM / AGEISM / RACISM (1)

1085 The Sunday newspaper magazine caters for women only. How sexist is that! Clearly, they don't receive complaints of sexism — or they choose to ignore them. It pisses me off.

*

1086 The same paper each Friday runs '10 Things To See, Hear And Do This Weekend.' Not one activity on the list ever caters for anyone over thirty. How ageist is that!

*

1087 A TV commercial has a smart Asian–Australian berating a dumb Aussie bloke over the latter's poor performing super fund. Imagine the outrage if the roles were reversed and the Asian–Australian was portrayed as the dumb-arse. (Footnote: I'm married to an Asian.)

*

1088 I'm still pissed how, as a young boy, my mother wouldn't let me play with the boy next door — because he was Catholic. (Footnote: I'm married to a Catholic. Mum would die!)

*

1089 I don't know if it's my age, but I'm paranoid about (1) being late, (2) my pension coming late, (3) a crane falling on me, (4) people who yell into their phone in public places.

*

1090 It beggars belief that women still get paid less than men. During my career, I sat on many interview panels, where good female candidates won over a male for no reason other than the organisation thought it could get away with paying the woman less of a salary.

*

1091 I used to attend my annual school reunion, but *health* and *marriage* problems were banned as topics of conversation. It left me with nothing to talk about, so I stopped going.

*

1092 Why isn't dentistry on Medicare, and why is Viagra so expensive? Both are essentials.

COMPUTER SPEAK

Today's computer language pisses me off. I so yearn for the days when ...

1093 *Acrobat* was what you found in a circus

1094 *chip* came with fish

1095 *password* was what you needed to gain entry to the smokers' den at high school

1096 *streaming* was about putting the bright kids in one class, dummies like me in another

1097 *bit* was a bite, as in 'my sister bit me'

1098 *RAM* was what sired forty lambs per year

1099 *content* was how good you felt

1100 *hardware* was something you bought in a shop which sold nuts and bolts

1101 *software* didn't mean anything

1102 *back-end* was a person's arse

1103 *boot* was a working man's shoe, or getting the sack

1104 *cloud* was the white stuff which hung in the sky (not exactly sure what it is now)

1105 *gateway* led to the chook house

1106 *mouse* was why you kept a cat

1107 *firewall* was a steel door which kept a fire from spreading to the boss's office

1108 *recycle bin* was, more recently, what you put out on Monday nights

1109 *cache* were the stolen goods you took to the pub to palm off, like a stuffed car

1110 *task manager* was a housewife

1111 *storage device* was a garden shed

1112 *Word* meant the Bible

1113 *keyboard* was found on a piano

1114 *docking station* had to do with NASA and satellites in outer space, and all that stuff

1115 *domain* was a man's shed out in the back garden

1116 *CAD* was a scoundrel

1117 *protocol* was Prince Philip walking three paces behind the Queen

1118 *bounce back* was what you did after you finished crying

1119 *tab* was where people spent all of their money on horses and dogs

1120 *cookie* was American for a sugar-laden biscuit

1121 *hard drive* was taking the kids on a holiday

1122 *boot* was where you stashed the kids while undertaking the hard drive

1123 *Quick time* was an excruciating, painful dance

1124 *joystick* was what the pilot used to steer the plane, or a topic in sex education classes

1125 *Java* was an island which belonged to Indonesia

1126 *utility* was a car with a tub at the rear used for carting dead and stricken sheep, and hay

1127 *file* was what you used to smooth out steel, or to manage your fingernails

1128 *motherboard* was what you shouted loudly when a shark bit your surfboard in half

1129 *virus* sent you to bed

1130 *spam* was canned food which was supposed to look like meat

1131 *zip* was on your pants and needed to be kept done up at all times

1132 *notebook* was what I write clever stuff in, clever stuff like this

1133 *dongle* was part of the male anatomy (see *joystick* above)

1134 *excel* described my writing (as in I excel at writing)

SEXISM, AGEISM, RACISM (2)

1135 To the waiter, *'May we please have some tap water?'* *'Sure,'* he replied. *'It's there on the bench.'* What if I'd been twenty-four, and female? Would the arsehole have fetched it for us?

HARD QUIZ

1136 *I'm pissed off that I never got to be on Hard Quiz. I failed the initial, online quiz. I'd been eager to be one of the four contestants to be ridiculed by host Tom Gleeson while I joyfully answered questions on my 'special subject', plus those on Tom's special subject. All of this while Tom did his level best to humiliate and belittle me. My special subject was to have been former prime minister, the late Malcolm Fraser. Here are the questions I would have expected to have been asked, along with my answers:*

1. For how many days was Malcolm Fraser 'caretaker' prime minister in 1975? *Thirty-two*

2. What degree did Fraser get at Oxford University? *Politics, Economics and Philosophy*

3. What is Tamie Fraser's maiden name? *Beggs*

4. Fraser is our fourth-longest-serving PM. Who served longer? *Menzies, Hawke, Howard*

5. What reason did Fraser give for resigning from John Gorton's cabinet? *Disloyalty*

6. At the time Fraser resigned from Gorton's cabinet, what portfolio did he hold? *Army*

7. In order of age, Fraser's four children are ... *Angela, Mark, Hugh and Phoebe*

8. From 1985–86, Fraser was chairman of what international body? *The Commonwealth Group of Eminent Persons against Apartheid in South Africa*

9. At the 1975 Federal election, the Fraser-led Liberal Party won a still-standing record number of how many House of Representative seats? *Ninety-one*

10. What two breeds of cattle did Fraser run at Nareen? *Hereford and Simmental*

11. Which two schools did Fraser attend? *Tudor House in NSW and Melbourne Grammar*

12. For which party was Fraser's father a senator from 1901–1913? The *Free Trade Party*

13. In what year was Malcolm Fraser made a Companion in the Order of Australia? *1988*

14. Why did Fraser sell Nareen in 1996? *Lloyds of London made a 'call' on its members*

15. In what years was Malcolm Fraser born, prime minister, died? *1930, 1975–83, 2015*

LIFE'S DREADS

I'm not at all embarrassed to admit how utterly terrified I am of having to do any of these:

1137 high-rise window cleaning (basically, anything to do with dangling from a rope)

1138 caving (the very thought of entering a cave causes me to shake like all get up)

1139 parachuting / hot air ballooning (what possesses people to do such stupid things?)

1140 shark cage diving (even with the metal grille window locked shut)

1141 running a marathon / running a sprint / running (unless it's because I'm late)

1142 riding a bull, steer or horse at a rodeo / running with the bulls (unbelievably stupid)

1143 breaking apart two fighting dogs

1144 whitewater rafting / travelling down any river which isn't dead calm and peaceful

1145 acting (in particular, having to learn lines, something I cannot do to save myself)

1146 paragliding / parasailing / skydiving / scuba diving / ziplining / abseiling / flyboarding

1147 bungee jumping / bungee jumping out of a hot air balloon

1148 heli-skiing / (even) riding in a helicopter causes shivers

1149 walking a tightrope — even if it's only one foot off the ground

1150 rock climbing (I'm already shaking at the thought; why on earth do people do it?)

1151 singing without the words in front of me

1152 walking on a suspension bridge (confession: *being* on any bridge sets me shaking)

1153 astronauting / lying on a bed of nails / drinking ouzo

1154 racing a car or motorbike / being the passenger in a racing car or on a motorbike

1155 playing poker or roulette — and seeing what little money I have disappear, quickly

1156 being up in one of those huge building site cranes — I'm shaking at the thought

1157 being up close to, and peering into a volcano

1158 eating haggis

1159 exercising

GREAT AUSTRALIAN

It pisses me off that adventurer and philanthropist Dick Smith isn't Governor-General.

1160 Because of his amazing contributions to Australian society. Dick has had many agendas, all with Australia's best interests at heart. Like saying our biggest taxpayers should be named and publicly thanked for their outstanding public service. Who could argue with that? What a great idea! Back when I was writing a book on philanthropy, Dick allowed me to interview him at his Sydney office. Unfortunately, the book on Aussie philanthropists didn't get up, but I had the privilege of spending an hour with the amazing man. Part of that interview is worth retelling:

MT: *What was your first ever act of philanthropic giving?*
DS: I received a letter from Dr Tony Kidman (Nicole's late father), a researcher at Sydney's University of Technology. In the letter he asked me for a $10,000 gift to further his research work. I felt terribly affronted to

receive his letter, and wondered why I'd been targeted. But in the end, I sent the money. It became the start of my philanthropic giving.

MT: *Who taught you to be a giver?*
DS: My parents were into all kinds of community support activities. They taught me. But I'm not special; I'm just a car radio installer. (He repeats the bit about 'being just a car radio installer' three times during our hour together.)

MT: *How much money do you give away each year?*
DS: A million dollars to tax-deductible causes; $200,000 to non-tax-deductible projects.

MT: *How many requests for money do you receive each month?*
Dick doesn't answer. Instead, he calls out to staff in the general office. 'How many requests for money do we get each month? Two hundred?' A female voice answers, 'You see two hundred; we don't show you the other four hundred.'

MT: *Are Australians generous?*
DS: No, we're not generous enough. I think the government should publicly list the nation's top twenty taxpayers, so we can all thank them. We need to change the culture.

MT: *Does any single gift you've given stand out in particular?*
DS: A woman, desperate to escape her abusive husband, wrote to ask for $600 to transport her disabled child's

disability apparatus. Dick gave me the woman's first name and phone number, so I could talk to her direct, but only after Dick called her to make sure it was okay. I made the phone call, and when I heard the woman's moving story, I cried. She also told me how, after moving the family to their new home, one day there was a loud noise outside the house. It was Dick, who'd flown his helicopter to visit them. *'My angel,'* as she described her benefactor, *'had come to visit — and take the kids for a joy ride in the helicopter.'*

Footnote: Dick's current cause is for Australia to have a Population Growth Plan.

ROLE MODEL

1161 Andy, of Hamish and Andy, attended the same school as my sons. Whenever Andy saw me, he would say, *'Hello, Mr Thornton'* in a charming and upbeat way. It made me think how well he was going to do in life. What pisses me off is that there are not more individuals in this world with such confidence, good character and an infectious personality.

TELEMARKETING

1162 'Hello. Is this you, Michael?'

'Yes,' I reply, eagerly. 'What have I won?'

'It's Betty from the 'Save The Possum Society.' Before we proceed, I need to tell you this call is being monitored for quality and training purposes.'

'I don't want this call monitored for quality and training purposes. I don't want this phone call for anything. Just tell me what I've won.'

'Michael, do you know how many possums are killed each year?'

'I couldn't give a possum.'

'Many thousands,' she says.

'Good,' I reply. 'I'm responsible for a good many of those killings.'

'Can I suggest an amount you might like to given to save a possum?'

'No, you definitely cannot. But what you can do is give me your mobile phone number so I can call you when you get home — and annoy the crap out of you.'

'Shall I put you down for say two hundred dollars?'

'Let's say zero dollars,' I reply. 'What are we having for dinner?'

'We have several payment options.'

'We've just suffered a family tragedy,' I say.

'Would you like to put the two hundred dollars on Visa or Mastercard?'

'Hang on, I think our house is on fire!'

'And your Visa card numbers are …?'

PETROL HEAD DAUGHTER

1163 My 34-year-old daughter is in a car club. I tell her she should be playing with dolls.

SCHOOL SCANDAL

This really pissed me off!

1164 A Melbourne mother did a radio interview in which she said her sensitive, year 7 son was raped by a year 12 boy during a school camp. She said the school's vice-principal admitted to *'knowing about'* the older boy, but had done nothing to investigate the incident, or punish the offender. The vice-principal hadn't said why no action had been taken. Two weeks after the mother did the radio interview, the school ran a huge newspaper advertisement for a new principal, to follow the present, retiring incumbent, who'd made … *'a magnificent contribution to the school and to education in general.'* The advertisement proclaimed the college to be a 'Child Safe School.' What a joke! The year 12 boy should have been charged. The boy *and his parents* should have been publicly named and shamed — and all three of them jailed. The vice-principal should have been sacked, and charged with wilful neglect, conspiracy, negligent duty of care, and every other possible jailable offence. The school should have been charged with false and grossly misleading advertising in relation to its ad for a new principal. Think about it. The older boy will go through life believing he can do whatever he wishes, with impunity, while the younger boy will be scared and most probably scarred — for life. One day the vice-principal will retire, and be told — and will believe — he'd made ... *a magnificent contribution to the school and to education in general.* Society never learns, and the mean and awful system in which we live pisses me off so much.

IMPORTANT ADVICE

1165 *'DON'T give her the ring until AFTER you've seen her mother with a head cold.'*

RETIREMENT

I'm mega pissed off how, since retiring, I no longer ...

1166 receive emails or phone calls offering lucrative consultancy work

1167 discover a subsequent, healthy consulting fee has landed in my bank account

1168 get an opportunity to work with some amazingly wonderful people

1169 can whinge about having to work with truly despicable people (three come to mind)

1170 get to indulge in long or even short, boozy work lunches and dinners

1171 feel wanted and valued — and told so to my face and in gushing notes of appreciation

1172 get to attend fully-paid conferences locally, interstate or overseas, especially overseas

1173 get to be a guest speaker at events — and receive accolades for my brilliant speeches

1174 get to mix with super important people, and them with me

1175 am told often that I have amazing, unique and irreplaceable skills (aw, shucks)

1176 receive a call from a head-hunter (well, it happened *once* in my fifty-year career)

1177 have an office with my name and title on the door

1178 have a desk with my name and title on a gold name plate

1179 have a fancy lapel badge with my name and title on it

1180 get to fly in a client's light plane (well, it happened *once* in my fifty-year career)

1181 get to stay in fabulous places, like New York's Hamptons (well, it happened *once*)

1182 get to hear and participate in juicy gossip at the office water cooler

OPINION POLLS

1183 It pisses me off that I've not been asked to participate in an opinion poll, during or after an election, when I have so much life experience, so much opinion to contribute.

UNCRICKETY

I continue to be pissed off about our once adored and adorable game of cricket.

1184 To the point of now watching it only occasionally, and only to remain informed! Apart from numerous acts of match-fixing on the subcontinent, two incidents involving our very own Australian cricketers leave me permanently pissed off. And no spin or weasel-words will change how I feel. Recently, I was on the tram, and I began to chat with a fellow passenger around my age. As the tram passed by the MCG, the topic of cricket came up. My fellow traveller told me how the 'Sandpapergate' incident had turned him off cricket — *for life*! I told him that I felt exactly the same way. In fact, we both felt disillusioned — and mightily pissed off. As a boy, I'd heard about and saw footage of the infamous 1932–33 'Bodyline' series: the nonstop bowling by English fast bowlers of short-pitched balls, designed to maim our batsmen. In 1935, the MCC — the home of world cricket — banned repetitive bouncers. Yet, Australia's two worst breaches of cricket morality continue to leave me gasping. In 1981, for the final ball of a match between Australia and New Zealand — with one ball remaining and New Zealand needing six runs to win — Australia's captain instructed his brother to bowl the final ball underarm — to dribble the ball along the ground, and thus make scoring the necessary six runs by the batsman impossible. Cricket legend, the late, great Richie Benaud, described the incident as the lowest act, ever. The second incident occurred in 2018, in Cape Town, South Africa. One of our bowlers, with the acquiescence of the team captain and vice-captain, used sandpaper to 'rough-up' a ball — to make it turn more in the air and thus make it harder for the opposing batsmen to hit. Like many Aussies who once loved our wonderful national game of cricket, I felt totally ashamed. Like my fellow traveller on the tram, I no longer care much for our once adored and compelling game of cricket. I often wonder what Richie would have said about Sandpapergate.

POLITICS

Things about politics which piss me off include...

1185 the arrogance and self-entitlement nature of the whole thing

1186 people who don't understand that a strong economy is the first rule of politics

1187 people who believe that a strong economy is the *only* priority in politics

1188 people who don't accept that Australia's defence comes second in importance

1189 people who don't understand that a 'centre' political platform is the only way politics will ever work successfully in Australia

1190 global warming and climate change deniers one day will apologise — it's not too late

1191 governments which belittle and persecute the poor, the needy and the vulnerable

1192 governments which clearly reward electorates which vote for them (sports rorts)

1193 politicians who treat voters as mugs, tell blatant lies, and feather their own nest

1194 politicians who don't know when it's time to make way for others to have a go

1195 politicians who don't have their salaries decided by a truly independent tribunal

1196 parliamentarians who don't answer the questions asked of them

1197 politicians who lack any kind of humility, integrity, good humour, common sense

1198 an otherwise good state government which (a) wilfully allocates taxpayers' funds for electioneering ['red-shirts'], without consequence; (b) seems hell bent on unionising the state's wonderful *volunteer* firefighting force [the CFA]; and (c) stubbornly refuses $4b of federal funding to build a cross-city tunnel [having already been forced to pay $1b compensation to a construction company for an earlier non-build of the very same tunnel]

WEIGHT LOSS

1199 I joined a swim club but lost nothing. I didn't know you need to get in the water!

INSTRUCTIONS

Being told to read instructions of any kind piss me off. Here are two scenarios ...

1200 Men, I freely confess, are hopeless with instruction manuals. This story goes back to 1972, when I was at agricultural college. One Friday, after lunch, we had a guest speaker from a rural supplies company. His talk was all rather ho-hum until he placed a big box on the front bench. He ripped open the lid, and removed what clearly was the instruction manual (in eleven languages). He then proclaimed, *'The first thing you do is this ...'* Whereupon, with one mighty heave, he threw the hefty volume out over the heads of a dozen students and out through an open window. It was a good thing his throw was good; had it not been, those boys would be dead! I've never forgotten the point that salesman made that day. Regrettably, to no lasting effect.

1201 Another time, we were given a written test. The question paper began ... *'Read through this whole paper before attempting your answers.'* Most of us ignored the instruction — naturally — and dived into question one. Those of us scribbling soon noticed something odd: several students were not writing; they were sitting with their hands on their head. One by one a scribbling student would call out a loud expletive, then he too would stop writing and put down his pen, place his hands on his head, and sit there, grinning. Those of us still writing answers didn't understand what was going on. Up front, the lecturer wasn't any help. He pretended to read a book. Common sense eventually prevailed, and I realised that whatever was going on had to be explained somewhere on the test paper. I did as we were first instructed; I went back to the start and began to read through the test paper, finishing at the final line, which read ... *'Disregard all of the above and place your hands on your head.'* Stupid me!

BULL RING

I first saw the game played in a pub in the outback — even though I couldn't master it myself.

1202 Bull Ring is amazing for its simplicity, precision and affordability. There are just four components: an eye screw, a piece of string, a hat peg, and a metal ring eight centimetres in diameter, like those in a bull's nose (hence the game's name). The eye screw is placed in the ceiling two metres out from a wall, the string then tied to the screw. The bull ring initially is tied loosely to the hanging string, then carried through its pendulum to the wall, so that, fully extended, the ring fits neatly over the hat peg, which is positioned on the wall at chin-height. The string is then tied off at that length. A player takes the bull ring to the other end of the pendulum, furthest from the wall. With the ceiling screw two metres from the wall, logically the outer end of the pendulum will be four metres from the wall. Holding the bull ring with a thumb and two fingers

— with arm fully extended — the player executes not a throw but a downward push left or right through the pendulum. The ring needs to be going past the hat peg — not hit it directly — so that it latches on. And here's the skill: once you get the knack of the game — and find your rhythm — you begin to understand the precision required. This way, endless 'hooks' can be achieved. Later, at the now long-gone Oxley pub in the NSW Riverina, I saw a rouseabout challenge a burly shearer to a game of ten 'throws' each. The bet: $100. Not a small sum for a shearer or young wool-table boy. The shearer went first. He found his 'spot' on which to stand, while a friend stood close to the hat peg to return the ring to the shearer each time he got it 'on.' With forty onlookers, the only sound in the pub was the gentle humming of the bar fridge. The shearer scored eight out of ten hooks. The boy then had his turn, and scored nineteen 'hooks' in a row; clearly, an expert! A wise older shearer caused a distraction while the boy, along with his winnings, were whisked out of town by his rouseabout mates — before the furious shearer could do him any harm.

RANDOM PISSERS (1)

1203 The only thing worse than not getting a thank you from the person you let out of the lift ahead of you is when she beats you to the hotel reception desk to settle her bill — and doesn't say to you, *'It was so kind of you to let me out of the lift ahead of you. You go first.'*

*

1204 Three university professors blew the whistle on their institution for enrolling unqualified students, to maximise tuition income. The professors cited an overseas student who was enrolled in a *MASTERS* of IT. He didn't even know what a USB stick is!

*

1205 It pisses me off how I can find my way *into* an IKEA store, but need help to get *OUT*!

*

1206 It pisses me off when someone joins a group in a queue ahead of me, claiming they're from the same family. *'Show me your birth certificates,'* I once said, and got serious stares.

*

1207 The talkback caller who began, *'I'll be quick ...'*; then droned on until he got dumped.

*

1208 The painful wait between sending a manuscript — and getting the rejection email!

RETAIL STAFF

1209 I handed the prescription to the pharmacy person, who studied it, then asked, *'You want this?'* 'No,' I said, *'I want you to see my doctor's cool handwriting. Of course, I want it.'* I took a seat. Then the pharmacist called me up. She asked for my date of birth. Clearly, the initial staff person hadn't thought to ask me for it. Indeed, I doubt that person thinks about very much at all. I took my seat, and said a short prayer for the future of the world.

WHY I HATE… [INSERT NAME]

1210 just because we went to the same school doesn't mean I have to like him

1211 because his father drove a Benz (and we had an old Holden), doesn't change things

1212 he wore an expensive watch; I didn't

1213 he was good at every sport while I was pathetic at everything

1214 he was always able to talk his way out of any kind of trouble; I got caned

1215 he was better looking and faster than me — and still is!

1216 he had a father to teach him stuff; I didn't

1217 he claimed to have bedded a girl during the annual school dance; I managed one kiss

1218 he got picked first for team games; I got chosen last, after the boy with the broken leg

1219 he knew how to work a chainsaw; I didn't

1220 he knew what a chainsaw is; I didn't

1221 he never got caught; I did

1222 teachers always smiled at him but scowled at me

1223 when I last saw him, he had all his teeth, while mine are being extracted one by one

1224 he was friends with the prefects and eventually became one; I hung out with losers

1225 after he inherited the family farm, he sold it for $30 million; I write

1226 he married into money; I married a school teacher's daughter

1227 he's a member of the Melbourne / Australian Clubs; I belong to 'roadside assistance'

1228 when we were in grade 5, Mum said the only way to stop him bullying me was to snot him in the nose, which I did. I shook for a week, but the bullying stopped

RIPPED OFF

1229 I ordered *free* sample pills online. I then clicked 'Go to checkout.' Postage was $289.

RANDOM PISSERS (2)

1230 A landowner wanted a power pole removed from the front of his new seaside holiday home, to give him an uninterrupted view of the ocean. He accepted the quote of $30,000 to have the pole removed. Trouble is, while the pole was being removed, local businesses lost a whole day of power, and all their perishables went off. The cost of the disruption to local businesses was $40,000. Businesses which complained were told to suck it up.

*

1231 One Friday night, a wealthy businessman posted a cheque for $500 to his local council. He knew that $500 was the maximum fine payable for cutting down trees without a council permit, permission he knew he was unlikely to be granted. At 5 the next morning, a bulldozer arrived and mowed down a grove of tall cypress trees, trees which hitherto were blocking his view of the sea. Fine paid; job all done and dusted.

1232 When I was eighteen, I spent a year working in a factory in England. One day, a supervisor asked me if I'd like to earn five hundred pounds. Of course I would — I was eighteen. He got me to meet him at lunchtime the following Monday in his car in the factory car park. He got me to sign two cheques (both with my name *pre-printed* on them). One was for ten thousand pounds, the other for twenty thousand. And he gave me my welcome five hundred quid.

1233 Part-time board members of a supermarket chain each get paid hundreds of thousands of dollars in directors fees, while the supermarket's fruit pickers get $14 per hour.

DREADED WORDS

1234 My cardiologist: *'You must do a stress test'* (struggling uphill on a fast-moving belt)

SOUTH SUDANESE

1235 The sad thing about the emergence of South Sudanese street gangs is that, deep down, Sudanese folk are honest, sincere and gentle people. I say this with some experience. I once spent a weekend in the impoverished town of Rumbek, which back then was the interim capital of the 'new' South Sudan. My then-wife worked for the United Nations, and I was 'allowed' to join her in what was an otherwise 'closed' country for a three-day weekend. During the weekend, we befriended a nineteen-year-old, ex-child-soldier, who'd fought against the North. David was applying to gain entry to a Ugandan university. He was a very determined, well-mannered and ambitious young man. We invited him into the UN compound for Sunday lunch. I'm sure he was hungry as all hell, but he waited until we were served before he took his turn at the buffet. For a tall nineteen-year-old, he ate sparingly. At the time, I recall wishing we could take him home with us to Australia — so he could attend a university here.

But such a dream was impossible. I blame the problem with Melbourne's teenage street gangs unequivocally on the boys' *fathers*. Many fathers shoot through, leaving exhausted mothers to raise a heap of kids. Mothers have no (physical) power over their teenage sons, whereas a strong father, if present in their sons' lives, could discipline them. And keep them off the streets at night. I applaud the efforts of South Sudanese community leaders, clergy and youth workers, who try their best, yet few outsiders can replace a tough father's influence — a strong male figure who could discipline a wayward teenage son. *Where are the fathers?* What are the courts and lawmakers doing to make fathers live up to their parental responsibilities? Or am I oversimplifying the problem?

LIES, LIES, LIES

1236 The Internet booking site says *'Only one room left.'* I pay for the room, then go back into the same website and same hotel room, to see if it's true. *'Only one room left.'*

CHARITABLE INTENTS

1237 I'm on a country bus, sitting up front. I overhear the banter between the driver and a boarding passenger. The 30-year-old doesn't have money for his fare, and asks to be allowed to pay later. Clearly, the driver isn't about to cut him any slack. So, I pay the $4 fare for him.

*

1238 Rather than tell the smiling, mature-aged supermarket checkout lady about my woes, I tell her she has a gorgeous smile. She beams at me, and I think I've made her day.

*

1239 An overseas friend, 24, emails to say she needs emergency surgery. She asks to borrow A$1,500. Her zeal in asking for the money is matched only by her fervent promises to repay the loan as soon as she gets well. The operation is a success and she secures a good job. Yet, after months of wellness and work, no repayment is forthcoming. I write to ask for a payment plan. Nothing happens. Two months later, a small instalment arrives. Four months later, there's a Facebook post with a photo of her on an overseas flight. I write to ask for another payment. No reply. My worry is, if I was asked again to help, I'd most likely do it. It's who I am. Eventually, she returns all of the loan. But not without a lot of asking.

*

1240 When my then-wife and I lived in New York, after dining at a pizza joint, we walked home, me with the remains of the pizza for my lunch the next day. We encountered Steve, a homeless guy, who lived under the elevated train track. *'Give him the pizza,'* said my wife. *'No way,'* I replied. *'It's tomorrow's lunch.' 'Give him the pizza!'* I did as I was instructed.

*

1241 Back to the guy on the bus. On several subsequent mornings he got on the bus at the same stop, and each and every time he walked straight past me without making eye contact or showing any interest in repaying the $4. Can you believe it? What would you do?

BOOK BORROWINGS

1242 Every so often I look online to see how many copies of my book — *Jackaroo* — are 'on loan' from Victoria's public libraries. Nineteen of the state's libraries have copies. When last I looked, libraries at Cobram, Traralgon and Wangaratta had copies out on loan. Sixteen other libraries didn't. What is *wrong* with people? It pisses me off, big time. The best I've had at any one time is eleven borrowings, but that was back when the book first came out. The federal government pays a royalty of $2.14 each time a copy is borrowed, and last financial year I had 331 borrowings. I've thought of driving around Victoria continually borrowing copies from libraries — to boost my royalty income. But the economics don't stack up when you take into account the cost of the petrol and accommodation. Nor, probably, does the law, or its intent. Instead, to boost my confidence, I check the current borrowings of a book by another author, a friend whose book launch I attended. The poor guy, who's thirty years younger than me, has only *one* copy of his book in the state's library system. I'm buoyed that I'm doing better than him! I then reflected that, rather than complain about my poor borrowings, I should rejoice in the knowledge that three generous souls — all total strangers — are reading my book. Instead of feeling angst, I'm learning to feel honoured to have any and all patronage. Plus, I receive lovely and kind emails from readers. It makes me realise how I must be more grateful for each and all of life's blessings, big and small.

PUTTING ON THE MOZZ

1243 I shouldn't watch sport on TV. Why? Because whenever I do, the team I follow begins to lose. I jinx my team every time I watch. So, in fairness to my team, I switch off. Later, I learn that my team has recovered, and won. Sad part is, I didn't get to see it happen!

LIFE'S LITTLE PROTESTS

I'm disappointed in myself that I no longer take risks and push boundaries.

1244 For example, there is something I find extremely courageous about sitting at a donut shop's *'customers-only'* table — eating a mandarin brought from home. One of life's little protests, so I've learned to believe, is knowing how far one can push a boundary, how far one can go without being caught — and being locked-up; things like …

*

1245 entering a hotel only to use its toilet

1246 using a café table not to buy their stuff, but to read my book and drink their free water

1247 using a petrol station rubbish bin to empty my car's rubbish, clean the windows, and pump up the tyres — but not to buy petrol

1248 doing the newspaper puzzles in the local public library instead of paying to photocopy the page, so others after me can do the puzzles, too

1249 snooping around outside a house that's for sale but not presently open for inspection

1250 jumping a queue — and remaining resolutely defiant

1251 ordering a dish that's not on the restaurant menu

1252 upon getting a car insurance quote, telling them I'm likely to drive two thousand kilometres per year when I know I will drive five times that distance

1253 transferring a parking ticket from one car's windscreen to another car's windscreen

1254 opening a door for, or paying a compliment to — and copping abuse from — a stranger

1255 paying for coffee and cake with coins of small denominations

1256 at the post office asking to see a sheet of stamps, then choosing the one in the middle

1257 telling a mother with badly-behaved children in a supermarket to discipline them

1258 telling someone he/she is good looking when we both know I'm lying

1259 asking a singer if he/she takes lessons

1260 knowing when to say nothing, and when to throw caution to the wind

QUIZ

Here's a quiz to piss you off:

1261 what is the naughtiest thing you've ever done? Did you get caught?

1262 what is the least kind thing you've ever said or done to someone?

1263 is there someone in your life you have never forgiven, and never will?

1264 when was the last time you told a lie, what was it, and to whom did you tell it?

1265 have you ever stolen anything, *anything* at all, ever?

1266 do you have an up-to-date will and enduring general and medical powers of attorney?

1267 is your will in any way contentious, and likely to be contested, but you don't care?

1268 have you ever been given too much change — and not given it back?

1269 name two people you would least like to be stuck with on a desert island for 30 days.

1270 have you ever cheated — even in the tiniest way — on your tax return?

1271 name the relative you least like. Does he/she know it?

1272 do you have any undeclared cash hidden anywhere?

1273 have you cheated at the supermarket self-checkout (including not scanning the bag)?

1274 have you ever not returned a supermarket trolley to a designated drop-off place?

1275 do you truly believe you are a generous person?

1276 do you truly believe you are not overweight?

1277 do you gamble, and, if so, what's been your biggest single loss?

1278 have you ever cheated, or attempted or been tempted to cheat on your partner?

1279 since you became an adult, have you ever poo-ed or wee-ed in your pants?

1280 have you ever knowingly and deliberately told your partner an untruth?

GIFTS

1281 have you ever 'gifted-on' a Christmas or birthday present — and been caught out?

WORRIES

Increasingly, as a 71-year-old baby boomer, I become pissed off worrying about the future.

1282 about my future, as well as that of other baby boomers.

1283 I used not to be like this — being scared, being a worrier — but now I find I quickly become maudlin when I think about the future of the world.

1284 our planet is warming, and we're having catastrophic droughts, floods and fires. As I write this, fires are raging all over eastern Australia. (What if the sun switches off!)

1285 I worry about the economy. Interest rates are at a record low, with almost no room to go lower. I fret for young families with huge mortgages, and what will happen to them when interest rates return to normal — say 7% or 12%. Young borrowers won't be able to pay their mortgage. There will be foreclosures left, right and centre. Families will be out on the street.

1286 with so much construction going on (experts gauge the state of the economy by the number of cranes in the sky), I worry what will happen when the cranes start to disappear.

1287 all of which leads me to a recurring nightmare, where the millennials round up all of us boomers, and place us in huge, bland dormitories, packing us away without any amenities — so we are no longer a drain on the nation's shrinking finances.

1288 baby-boomer politicians will get to live in posh facilities if they agree to go quietly.

1289 in my awful dream, we can choose to stay and live on as vegetables, or be euthanised.

1290 most boomers will choose the latter.

1291 there'll be no need for pensions; our superannuation will pay for our dormitory bed.

1292 'Generation Brave' will have taken over the world.

1293 if you don't believe me, consider this: 40% of adult children currently have their weekly groceries paid for by their (ageing) parents; 20% have their petrol paid for by their (ageing) parents. Consider what will happen when these ageing parents decide they either no longer *wish* to pay these bills, or no longer *can* pay them. The millennials will come after us.

BELIEVE IT OR NOT

It happened in the seaside hamlet of Kettering, south of Hobart; I'm pissed that I missed it.

1294 in February, 1976, a 39-year-old man was woken by his child, crying. He then noticed through the window what appeared to be a plane coming down from the eastern sky. A widespread glow surrounded the sight. Thinking it might be a plane accident, the man hurried towards the light, dressed in his dressing gown. From a small rise, he had a clear view some thirty metres down the slope, from where he saw a dome-shaped object parked. Windows on the object gave off a bright light. The exterior, he later told others, looked like it was made of aluminium. Below the windows, a small ledge led to the base, with a short, vertical side. Through a window, the man saw a tall, cylindrical object, which he likened to a ship's compass mounting, and motionless grey shapes, which looked like car seats with head rests seen from behind. He thought there may have been 'entities' sitting in the seats. As he drew closer, he heard a humming noise, like an electric motor. Then the object rose from the ground, its noise increasing. It lifted off slowly, then increased its speed. The object soon became a dot in the sky, and then disappeared. The whole incident lasted less than seven minutes, the man told reporters. He returned to the site the following morning and found that the grass where the object had been sitting was completely scorched. By the time authorities arrived, the scorched area was far greener than elsewhere. Investigators revealed no significant differences in the thermo-luminescent content of the soil and mineral particles taken from the surrounding area. The patch of grass later died. The investigating analyst concluded that the death of the grass was not due to substantial heating of the soil, neither was it caused by large doses of ionising radiation. So, what was it? The authorities didn't — or wouldn't — say. Which only goes only to piss me off even more.

A RAFT OF PISSERS (2)

More things I wish I could ban, change, reverse, stop — or encourage and reward:

1295 pneumonoultramicroscopicsilicovolcanoconiosis

1296 I wonder if billionaires ever think about people who struggle, and what their immediate next thought is

1297 the menu said 'eggs' yet I found just *half of one* in my Caesar Salad

1298 the menu said 'anchovies' yet I found just *half of one* on my pizza

1299 the amazing relief which comes after the Microlax kicks in

1300 people to see, faces to paint

1301 anyone who says bushfires are God's revenge for same-sex marriage and abortion

1302 decades of bible-bashing evangelists sent by Australian churches to Pacific islands to brainwash local populations into believing God is vengeful, not loving

1303 people who end sentences with 'and that', as in *'There was a lot of smoke and that'*

1304 people who end sentences with 'wot-not', as in *'There was a lot of smoke and wot-not'*

1305 people who end sentences with 'eh', as in *'There was a lot of smoke, eh!'*

1306 hugely stressed I would receive a 'robodebt' letter demanding a massive repayment

1307 goals to achieve

1308 more goals to achieve

1309 struggling to achieve endless goals

1310 giving up on trying to achieve more goals

1311 *'I did not have sexual relations with that woman'*

1312 doing a Bill Clinton

1313 *'I have no recollection of ever meeting this lady'*

1314 doing a Prince Andrew

1315 *'I am not a crook'*

1316 doing a Richard Nixon

1317 *'I want to do you slowly'*

1318 doing a Paul Keating

1319 *'Embittered, miserable ghosts'*

1320 doing a Malcolm Turnbull

1321 *'Read my lips'*

1322 doing a George H. W. Bush

1323 overused quotes which everyone is totally sick of hearing

1324 'stray-ya' (for Australia)

1325 'nucular' (for nuclear, thanks to George W. Bush)

1326 *'Come From Away'*

1327 anyone who comes from anywhere is coming from away

1328 erectile dysfunction

1329 incontinence

1330 40% of English teachers say they are ill-equipped to teach English

1331 a cricketer says in future he needs to be careful using homophobic slurs. Really? Clearly, he doesn't get that it's not what one *says* but what one *thinks*

1332 Australians spend $400 million annually on unwanted Christmas presents

1333 council by-laws which forbid removal of highly combustible dead timber from roadsides

1334 *'Material, spiritual and emotional success is closer than you think'*; I wish

1335 a monthly direct debit falls on Sunday, so the cheeky biller takes my money on Friday

1336 can the annoying children in the Family Peace ads spell 'consequence' or 'tantrum?'

1337 you can always appeal to a higher authority

1338 given the delicacy of the human brain, what does that say about boxing/soccer/rugby?

1339 News Ltd — the first online news agency which wanted payment for news, so I didn't

1340 the company for which I worked — and to which I offered (free) advice on how to get more, much-needed *good* publicity — continually losing out to a Sydney rival

1341 the company for which I worked and offered (free) PR advice, fobbing me off

1342 one is too many, a thousand is not enough

1343 my mother told me never to talk to strangers, which made for a very lonely childhood

1344 it is so much better and easier on the ears when the band takes a break

1345 when Kass steals food off my plate — it's a Filipino thing, but annoying as all get up

1346 news report: *'Italian council chamber floods moments after the council votes down measures to combat climate change'*

1347 the only *two* responses ever required in church are 'Yes' or 'Jesus'

1348 a petrol station asks if I want chocolates, but a chocolate shop never asks if I want petrol

1349 twenty-three former fire chiefs warn, *'This (fire threat) is different'* — falls on deaf ears

1350 twenty-three former fire chiefs ask three times to meet the prime minister — nah!

1351 news report: 'Cory Bernadi To Leave Politics;' shattering, heart-breaking news

1352 sticky-beaking

1353 rubber necking

1354 I'm puzzled how our sewage goes uphill to get to Werribee

1355 I'm puzzled how fresh water comes uphill to get to our place

1356 I'm puzzled as to where grey water goes, and how it gets there

1357 I'm puzzled as to what possesses me to eat dim sims; okay, *and* potato cakes

1358 regrets on the morning after

1359 worrying I'll look older than the other grandparents at next week's Grandparents' Day

1360 worrying I won't win the 100-metres dash at next week's Grandparents' Day

1361 I've never trusted the proposed religious discrimination bill — the right to discriminate

1362 I've been proved correct about the religious discrimination bill — it *will* discriminate

1363 guerrillas are fighters, gorillas are apes; guerrilla-gorillas must be fighting apes

1364 the US TV station which shows a burning log fire all day long on Christmas Day

1365 cinemas which turn on the heating to make patrons buy more cold soft drinks

1366 Michelle Obama's memoir has sold 12 million copies; mine sold 8,000

1367 the NDIS CEO reportedly gets $700,000 a year, which business commentators justify as comparable to other CEOs — which makes it one sick and never-ending *upwards* spiral

1368 I seem to have mislaid my Nobel Prize for Literature?

1369 Maria Von Trapp

1370 Mother Superior

1371 'Climb Every Mountain'

1372 Australia is the world's biggest consumer of beetroot

1373 quid-pro-quos

1374 bonhomie

1375 exactly *who* is responsible for *not* putting an apostrophe in The Presidents Cup

1376 the demise of the apostrophe

1377 willing a footballer to say, 'Please don't pay me that much because, given the total salary cap, I'd be taking money from young guys starting out and/or the women's team'

1378 sadness, anxiety and depression

1379 Electroconvulsive Therapy (ECT)

1380 mindfulness therapy

1381 'The Happiness Trap'

1382 Dr Russ Harris, author of 'The Happiness Trap', saying we can never always be truly happy; instead, we need to learn how to live with *unhappiness*

1383 Acceptance and Commitment Therapy (ACT)

1384 does Dynamic Lifter work the same as Viagra?

1385 the stupid TV ad where the silly woman throws a perfectly good leg of ham off a cliff!

1386 to Channel 10's 'The Living Room': since when did 'icypole' become 'popcycle?'

1387 to the ex-member for Higgins, Kelly O'Dwyer: since when did 'start' become 'get-go?'

1388 I was an hour out of JFK when the Twin Towers fell — we got dumped in Chicago

1389 Chicago police slogan: *'Our day starts when yours ends'*

1390 managing my non-existent share portfolio

1391 the price of gold

1392 punch-ups on talk shows

1393 Victorians on average swear five times a day, damn it

1394 boneless bananas

1395 cheese with bone-in

1396 'Store Wide Sale — Exclusions Apply'

1397 'Was $149, Now $148.99'

1398 Mexican waves

1399 advertisement: *'We've got braille products you've never before seen'*

1400 the extraordinary number of beauty pageant contestants committed to world peace

1401 book clubs which discuss novels only, when what I write is non-fiction, mostly

1402 sanitary pads on special for Father's Day

1403 moustache enhancer lotion on special for Mother's Day

1404 after searching the long-term car park for an hour, I found my car in the short-term park

1405 the courtesy bus to the terminal races past my stop four seconds before I get there

1406 *'There was no venom between Peter (Dutton) and I ...'* No, Prime Minister, it's 'Peter and me' — 'Peter and I' at the start of a sentence, 'Peter and me' at the end of a sentence; take out the 'Peter and' and it makes sense ['Plots and Prayers,' by Niki Savva]

1407 China accounts for 27% of world emissions; USA 15%; India 7%; Russia 5%; Australia 1.07%

1408 we must do our bit to stop global emissions (i.e. 'take out' China, the US and India)

1409 a third person has unfriended me

1410 the Anglican Church is sure to find a way to block *blessings* of same-sex marriages

1411 finally decided to put our framed Michael Jackson print out with the next hard rubbish

1412 two patrons leave the cinema having spent $57; they look thoroughly miserable

1413 I meant to enter the electrical store but instead stepped into Sexyland by mistake; should've gone to Specsavers

1414 sweating, because my Myki card is out of juice and I'm already on the tram

1415 I know. I will sit near the back door and jump off the tram if ticket inspectors come on board

1416 if I get run over jumping off the tram, it will have been the inspectors' fault that I died

1417 the cost of a funeral

1418 reports of a $3 billion blowout on the $11 billion Victorian Metro Rail Project

1419 reports of a budget blowout at home: can we afford $110 fake grass on the balcony?

1420 news headline: 'Prince Andrew Flees To Ecuador Embassy'

1421 setting aside pangs of false modesty, I truly believe I am the right person to lead any or all of the big banks out of their continuing quagmires

1422 having to add to the household budget regular dry cleaning — due to dribbles

1423 *'Did someone say KFC?'*

1424 knowing that the owner of the online hotel booking app is loafing on a Cabana beside a pool in Florida, cocktail in hand, hearing his phone go cha-ching every other second

1425 why must 'he or she' now be 'they?' It even sounds stupid

1426 forgetting who paid last time (and consequently paying more often than I ought)

1427 Martin Sheen (*'The Way'*, directed by Emilio Estevez) copied my every step on the Camino de Santiago de Compostela; but then I too copied the steps of 60 million before me

1428 staff at my personal café weren't paid overtime on a recent public holiday — I know because I asked one — but I'm unable to say anything to the lousy owner because (a) the staff member would get the boot for telling me, and (b) nothing will change anyway

1429 the department store staff member who said, *'May I suggest Sir tries "High & Mighty" in Little Collins Street?'* (better, I guess, than being told to try *"Low & Lousy"*)

1430 including dependencies, Australia in summer has *nine* different time zones

1431 eating sweetened condensed milk straight from the tube — until it's *all* gone!

1432 every hour *seven* Australians suffer a heart attack; that's one every nine seconds

1433 Americans don't use proper English (e.g. traveled, color, neighbor, apartment, cell phone, hood-for-trunk, candy, closet, cookie, subway, pacifier, vacation, zip code)

1434 news report: 'Councillors Take Bribes!'; no, that couldn't possibly be true, surely

1435 writer's advice to other writers: *'Stop wasting good writing time staring at Facebook'*

1436 learning that my son and his family were about to holiday in Vanuatu — by reading about it on Facebook (serves me right; I should have been writing, *not* staring at Facebook)

1437 missing our houseboat, enormously (but not missing the associated costs)

1438 I have successfully sussed out which houseboat to buy the minute we win lotto

1439 real estate agents who use a secret, wide-angle camera lens to make rooms look bigger

1440 wearing tracksuit pants to places I shouldn't (the right of every pissed-off old fart)

1441 *'You take the high road and I'll take the low road, and I'll get to choose my bunk bed before you'*

1442 who was this Winx person, anyway?

1443 PR firm to Prince Andrew: *'Take up cricket, score a hundred, and all will be forgiven'*

1444 smiling at 8 am as I watch folk leave our building for work, when *I don't have to*

1445 kept on hold for 40 minutes, *then* being told, 'I'll put you through to that department'

1446 when horses 1, 2 & 3 come 7th, 8th & 9th

1447 my age pension *isn't* indexed in line with the rising cost of a vanilla slice

1448 my superannuation pension is indexed to run out in 132 months

1449 being kissed on the lips by anyone other than Kass

1450 I hired a waste bin but neighbours filled it with their junk before I could with mine

1451 the link between my dentist wanting to extract my teeth, and his children's school fees

1452 trying to talk to a young person who's wearing headphones

1453 trying to talk to a young person

1454 how I loathe people who are glass-half-empty

1455 how I loathe myself when, from time to time, I slip into a glass-half-empty mood

1456 nincompoops who can't fight their way out of a paper bag

1457 nincompoops who can't fight at all, but who are in parliament

1458 nincompoops who keep trying to get into parliament

1459 my late Yorkshire-born grandfather, who used 'pillock' to describe a nincompoop

1460 daughter: *'Love you ten dollar, daddy'*

1461 daughter: *'Love you to China and back, daddy'* (on second thoughts, make that *Singapore*)

1462 daughter: *'Love you one dollar, daddy'*

1463 I know; let's put a safe injecting room next door to that primary school

1464 each week, 144 Australians give up smoking

1465 each week, tens of thousands of Australians don't give up smoking, but say they will

1466 *'The lady is not for turning'*

1467 doing a Maggie Thatcher

1468 the monthly household budget says $40 is available for Wellbeing, and I can't decide between a bottle of whisky or gin

1469 an hour spent in Bunnings is better than an hour with my psychologist — and it's free

1470 back when we had a farm, I built a chook house — during its life it cost $45 per egg

1471 back when I was a jackaroo for Malcolm Fraser, I came across a stricken ewe trying to give birth; I rummaged inside and found twins: one alive, one dead

1472 back when I was a jackaroo for Malcolm Fraser, I found a stray lamb which needed to be castrated; I said to Mr Fraser, *'Do you want to bite them out, or shall I?'*

1473 advertisement: *'If you can prove in the High Court of Australia* [approx. $100,000 per sitting day] *that you've found a price lower than ours, we will beat it by ten per cent'*

1474 the huge cost, disappointment and tears of the sixteen days that are an Olympic Games

1475 the journalist who wrote, 'outside of Melbourne'; what's with the 'of' bit; pathetic

1476 why do I always carry my phone when (a) I know for a fact that Kass is at home, asleep, and (b) my kids never call, anyway? (And because I'm old, no one else ever calls me)

1477 the Walton (Walmart) family, it's said, makes A$101,000 a minute; Amazon's owner A$216,000 a minute

1478 two tomatoes have emerged on the vine on our balcony

1479 the best way to put a full, tied-off kitchen bag into a required second bag is to hold the filled bag by what teeth I still have (Is this clear? Do you require additional explanation?)

1480 update: the Michael Jackson print has been dispatched to the basement storage cage

1481 being out after 10 pm

1482 having known only trumpet 'buttons', learning to use a trombone 'slide' in two days

1483 playing Colonel Bogey on my new trombone in a street march three days later

1484 what we call Christmas Stockings, Filipinos call Santa Socks

1485 a pile of fresh bird poo on my car's roof within seconds of leaving the car wash

1486 trying desperately to remember the name of my first love

1487 trying desperately to remember the names of my subsequent loves

1488 after remembering them, trying desperately to forget the names of all past loves

1489 giving out one's visa card numbers online has to be the silliest thing one could ever do

1490 Q. 'Hey Siri, do I look old?' A. 'I don't have an opinion on that'

1491 Q. 'Hey Siri, how old are you?' A. 'I'm as spry as a slice of young ginger'

1492 Q. 'Hey Siri, what pisses you off?' A. 'It wouldn't be nice to tell you that'

1493 each week, 2,000 more cars are added to Melbourne's roads

1494 fit, young pedestrians who have the temerity to overtake me on the footpath

1495 news report: 'Courageous granny hunts down

granddaughter's rapists and, despite their pathetic pleas for mercy, she shoots off their genitals'

1496 stiff cheddar

1497 bakeries which no longer sell a 'baker's dozen'

1498 in the first 12 months after the law was enacted, 6,538 same-sex couples were married — and we were one of them

1499 people in the country stop and say hello; people in the city walk with their head down

1500 at the nursing home I visit each week, today's memorial service for a recently departed resident will be followed at 4 pm by 'Casino Corner', life goes on, regardless

1501 'passed' will always be 'passed away' to me

1502 Halloween is un-Australian

1503 Thanksgiving is un-Australian

1504 Black Friday 'sales' not only is un-Australian, it is supposed to commemorate the tragic loss of life in the 1939 bushfires, not some jumped-up, crass, American shopping spree; Shaver Shop, Hardly Normal, et al., ought to be ashamed of yourselves

1505 parents who push their academically-and-sports-gifted child into a (limited-tenure) career in sport, when the teenager is smart enough to become a heart surgeon — for life

1506 advertisers which extol the *who* and *what* of a product, but never the *how* and *why*

1507 thank goodness for SBS News for presenting real world news, not local car prangs

1508 outfits which sell stuff *only* online, and downplay the postage and handling charges

1509 why are weekend-only drivers so hopelessly incompetent?

1510 of all the important news stories available across the globe, why does our highest rating radio station lead with someone who burned his hand?

1511 having a fragrance strip dangling from your rear vision mirror can put you over .05

1512 beetroot has been getting terrible press of late

1513 everywhere else in the world, hotel checkout is at noon

1514 I believe I would make a most engaging and interesting panellist on 'QandA'

1515 politician: *'We've had a few untidy days, but I remain focused on policy'*

1516 may we please have a progress report on the swamp, wall, 'locking her up', and *'lots-and-lots of fries'*

1517 after much consideration and following a lifetime of personal patronage, I've decided I'm willing for the Werribee sewerage plant to be named 'The Michael Thornton Poo Farm'

1518 I wonder what it's like to be up on 1,171 charges, whether I'd sleep at night

1519 in its day, Holden turned out 780 cars a day; today, not one

1520 US fashion show promotes merino wool — except the sheep shown are Corriedales

1521 US Scouts Inc. files for bankruptcy due to the cost of historical sexual abuse claims

1522 murderers who get away with manslaughter

1523 'jump online' — a thoroughly stupid call; I have no intention of jumping on anything

1524 after much consideration, I'm willing to accept fame and tell my story for $750,000

1525 the big banks are so ingrained, no punishment will make them change their ways

1526 'blooding'

1527 fast-food joints which fill a cup with ice, then top it off with a thimble-full of fizz

1528 radio promotions to which I dutifully register — from which I never win a brass razoo

1529 we never hear about *overpayments* to employees; funny, that

1530 wasabi, or what purports to be — and later trying to recover from it

1531 Y is a place in France

1532 oh, how I miss riding the Tea Cups at Disneyland

1533 800 million cars are manufactured worldwide each year

1534 Australians who live to seventy have a 66 per cent chance of contracting skin cancer

1535 a 'survivor' appears on *The Project* — I cannot understand a single word she says

1536 MP says he will never download TikTok to his phone — that's enough warning

1537 people who, things which

1538 I just read some of these gripes to Kass, and she said, *'I don't think it's going to sell'*

1539 no news is good news

1540 any publicity is good publicity

1541 prediction: by 2024 *all* major sport (cricket/footy/tennis) will be *only* on Pay TV

1542 prediction: by 2025 ABC TV will run advertisements

1543 prediction: by 2026 commercial, free-to-air TV will be history

1544 I apologise for having carried on like a two-bob-watch, Bob

1545 my father died at forty-eight; sister at fifty-four; mother at eighty-nine; son at twenty-eight; reaching seventy-one is good

1546 don't strive to add more years to your life; strive to add more life to your years

1547 what have I missed?

1548 my embarrassing deathbed confession ... (you'll have to wait for it)

1549 my eulogy is ready for release

1550 I've prepared a list of things Kass and the kids will need to do when I cark it

1551 I got my mother's probate granted in just sixty days of her dying

1552 despite my Liberal upbringing (read brainwashing), I've come to realise there are loonies on both the Left and the Right

1553 dreams of staying several nights in Kass's cousin's gorgeous cottage on a remote island in the Philippines — with a never-ending daily supply of fresh fish

1554 woops, I nearly repeated a gripe here

1555 things for which I'm grateful: 1. breath, 2. virus-free, 3. solvent, 4. happy, 5. loved

1556 helping daughter Mel (who is blind) to fill out forms (yet again) for her disability insurance claim (already approved); anything for an excuse to spend time with her, yeh!

1557 what can be done to stop so many murders? Clearly, current strategies aren't working

1558 insanely jealous that my son taught himself to play the piano

1559 JoshFromAccounts lauds Reagan and Thatcher's cruel economic and social policies

1560 when public speaking used to bring on severe back pain, but doesn't anymore

1561 'Farmer wants a wife' is like a meat market, so grossly embarrassing — all that's missing is the town square stage on which to parade the women slaves

1562 when I was a journalist and editing press releases sent in by PhD 'experts', I'd swap the first and final paragraphs, and the story would then make sense

1563 Channel Ten's *The Project* not only hits rock bottom by interviewing a football streaker (later fined $8,000), it promotes his GoFundMe page to help pay his fine (page raises $350)

1564 having a Senior Coach-in-waiting sitting next to the Senior Coach must make things awkward for both of them

1565 the young staff member who was made to say 'amount of customers' (instead of number) in the Bunnings TV ad

1566 I'd be worried too if a 94-year-old waved a sharp sword around my neck — even if she was the Queen

1567 can never get enough snorkelling

1568 people who change their football club allegiance — and then deny they ever followed the first team

1569 Hawthorn has gone to crap; thinking more and more about switching to St Kilda

1570 my first boss told me I could learn something even from a street sweeper in Collins St

1571 I think about owning a motorhome — and becoming a bald nomad — then images of outback murders on highways kick in and I drop the whole silly idea

1572 it's what the packaging doesn't say that has me worried

1573 one-third of the world's food gets thrown out

1574 the brother of a contestant should not be a judge, especially if that contestant wins

1575 one not only needs to be clean; one needs to be seen to be clean

1576 report: in the '70s: a 17-year-old claims how in Ballarat, after agonising over it for several days, he knocked on the door of the priests' house to report paedophilia, only to be told by a now well-known priest who answered the door to *'go away'*

1577 I wonder what it's like to be in a pickle

1578 do people who give odds in betting ads think they're adding in a positive way to society?

1579 more Karens

1580 more submarines

1581 more Big Brother

1582 The Palace Letters — what an anticlimax

1583 'He got beat'

1584 my bad

1585 'Bob's your uncle' (no he's not, he's my brother)

1586 there it goes being said again (on radio this time): 'amount of workers'

1587 Chinese Christians made to replace images of Christ with photos of President Xi

1588 around 1901, 2,500 Indian labourers died, most of them eaten by lions while they were building the Mombasa-Nairobi-Lake Victoria railway line

1589 Fox News' Chris Wallace interviews Trump — asks him to count back in 7s from 100 (gosh, how brave was that!)

1590 Lee Mack and David Mitchell on TV's *Would I lie to you?*

1591 Frank Sinatra learned to control his breathing by swimming laps underwater

1592 Frank Sinatra stopped an orchestra midway through a rehearsal, saying, '*Someone played a b-flat*'; a violinist raised her hand to admit her mistake

1593 Pistol, Barnaby and Boo

1594 Andy Griffith's 1953 sketch 'What It Was, Was Football'

1595 ABC TV screens an episode of a new show, but it was one which was made at least twenty years ago, because the NYC Twin Towers are seen standing in the background

1596 I purchased a packet of naan at the supermarket expecting it to be restaurant quality, but it tasted like shoe leather

1597 my essay 'The Agony and Ecstasy of a Would-be Writer' is now available free of charge for budding writers

1598 Twitter invites me to 'follow' Kanye West; who?

1599 profit-driven nursing home owners have so many serious questions to answer

1600 I heard Ellen is quitting

1601 I heard Elton is quitting

1602 447,000 Australians suffer from dementia; 250 new cases are diagnosed every day

1603 where was I?

1604 the childish and embarrassing 75 minutes which is parliamentary Question Time

1605 I've decided to start fossicking for gold; standby for a major announcement

1606 when no one was looking, I read an article about electric motor scooters

1607 news item: 'Louis Vuitton buys Tiffany & Co. for $23.9 billion'

1608 news item: 'This writer's jewellery empire is on the market for $23.90'

1609 a motoring magazine explains how to cook steak, and gives tips for better sleep

1610 Australians who go anywhere near drugs in Asia

1611 Australians who go anywhere near drugs, anywhere

1612 desperately wanting to give each teenager at the local skate park a good book to read

1613 how about funding the full-page corporate 'apology' ads from the CEO's salary?

1614 7,000 Lindt chocolate balls are eaten worldwide every minute

1615 132 million Coca-Cola drinks are consumed worldwide every minute

1616 still waiting to get a mention in the newspaper gossip column

1617 Q. When one solitary person holds the balance of power in the Australian parliament, whose ear does she have and what concessions does she get in return for her vote?

1618 A. *'Nothing to see here'*

1619 people who keep their bag on the seat next to them even when the train is full

1620 two houses either side of a long-stalled, local house build are for lease; something's up

1621 oh, Willy, all those lonely, lonely nights

1622 minister overrules panel, awards $100 million in grants to her own party's electorates

1623 illuminated, scrolling message machines on trains which say we're about to arrive at a station seven back from where we are presently

1624 so wish Barry Jones, eighty-seven, would go on Hard Quiz

1625 twelve students crammed into appallingly tiny dog box accommodation designed for two students

1626 they wouldn't let me sit on Santa's lap

1627 saving to dine at Florentino (at someone else's shout)

1628 saving to dine at Flower Drum (with a property developer bearing bags of cash)

1629 saving to dine at Vlado's — for the steak

1630 saving to dine at McDonald's — for the budget

1631 Thirty per cent of young people steal toilet paper from work

1632 bees which die after having sex — happily

1633 *Truth* newspaper's most famous headline: 'Sir Billy Died On The Job'

1634 how they put meat dishes last at the buffet, after you've filled your plate with salad

1635 Mr Bean's visit to the dentist

1636 any movie trailer which includes a gun

1637 movie trailers which make a film look appealing

but which don't repeat the name of the movie at the end of the trailer, making it impossible for old farts like me to remember it

1638 movie trailers, after which I whisper, *'Won't be bothering with that one!'*

1639 movie trailers, after which I whisper, *'Yep, put that one on the list to see'*

1640 a fellow past student travels to our school reunion lunch in his light plane

1641 I travel to our school reunion lunch on the No.96 tram

1642 *'Sunshine on my shoulders makes me happy / Sunshine in my eyes can make me cry'*

1643 the bank customer six in front who presents a calico bag containing 5,000 coins

1644 the demise of the $1 and $2 bank notes — and soon the $5 notes

1645 not realising I needed to take a ticket

1646 *'Well may God save the Queen, because nothing will save the Governor-General'*

1647 doing a Gough Whitlam

1648 the heart-breaking tragedy which is South Australia's missing Beaumont children

1649 the heart-breaking tragedy and aftermath that was the loss of Azaria Chamberlain

1650 being halfway there (3,300 gripes divided by 2 equals 1,650; got it?)

1651 still only two tomatoes have emerged on the balcony vines, but I'm willing more on

1652 the hair on the back of my left ear which I know is there but which I can't get at

1653 our quarterly electricity bill is $124 (no solar), but my life's goal is to get the bill down even lower while still being able to wash, run this laptop, and heat a can of Pal

1654 snake handlers

1655 elderly folk who, *unlike* me, are unable to pay their household bills online

1656 pill testing at music festivals

1657 drongos who don't use the pill testing facility at music festivals

1658 snake handlers who pull me from the crowd to have a python wrapped around my neck (what was I possibly thinking?)

1659 police officer: *'Good afternoon, driver; may I see your licence, please'*

1660 me: *'Hi there, officer. Hey, my daughter-in-law is a Member'*

1661 officer (sternly): *'Sir, do you know you were doing 44 in a 40 zone?'*

1662 me (sensing that using my daughter-in-law's status isn't working): 'No, officer'

1663 officer (handing me the penalty notice): 'You can pay this directly, or go to court'

1664 me (contritely): 'Thank you, officer; thank you very much'

1665 memo to Benjamin Law: 'Hey, Benjamin, I'm available any time to do Dicey Topics; you won't need to roll the dice; I'll just take "Sex", "Politics" and "Death" (in that order)'

1666 waiting to be asked to be the near-naked stud on a front cover of a men's magazine

1667 wondering which is my better side to be the near-naked stud on the front cover

1668 banks which oppose independent regulators being placed permanently on their staff

1669 bodies which investigate themselves, and *always* report, 'Nothing to see here'

1670 a royal commission into any authority which is told, 'Nothing to see here'

1671 a royal commission into the cosy, sweetheart-deal, auditing profession

1672 cease all activity with China (trade, education, etc.): short-term pain, long-term gain

1673 compulsorily acquire all land and businesses we've already given away to China

1674 banish Chinese intelligence operatives from Australia

1675 'Hey, Ashleigh, do you really need to stoop to Bartymite?'

1676 LGBTIQ ambassadors, warriors, champions, supporters — who never tire of battle

1677 badly needing to see my chiropractor — and it's Sunday

1678 news report: 'One in six deaths in nursing homes are unnatural'

1679 being *pressured* to give information is not the same as *pressurising* a can of fizz

1680 she is the youngest of three, or she is the younger of two; get it right, people

1681 I so wish I could draw and paint — and write

1682 my letter to the editor wasn't published, again

1683 my good friend's letter to the editor *was* published

1684 my last book wasn't published

1685 two books by good friends *were* published

1686 no, Damien Fleming (cricket commentator), it's *number* of people, not *amount*

1687 my mother told me that Australia in winter has more snow-covered area than the whole of Switzerland, but I didn't believe her until I read it on the Internet

1688 reading on the Internet that Australia has the

world's longest fence (5,530 km), although I swear I saw a hole in it, in the movie 'Rabbit Proof Fence'

1689 being told by my son that Australia has the world's longest stretch of dead-straight railway track (475 km); I tried counting but I fell asleep watching it go by

1690 slow TV on SBS

1691 people who experience incredible luck

1692 people who never experience misfortune

1693 people who always appear to be happy

1694 people who never appear to be unhappy

1695 cold pizza

1696 cold tea

1697 cold apartment

1698 hot beer

1699 hot pants

1700 hot apartment

1701 Q. Is it possible for a citizen, or a group of citizens, to pursue a class action against one or more politicians for irresponsible governance and dereliction of electoral duty in regard to their inaction over accepted science in relation to climate change?

1702 sad there'll be no more 110 km, four-day, teenage hikes in Victoria's high country

1703 sad there'll be no more smoking tea leaves rolled up in dunny paper during those teenage hikes in Victoria's high country

1704 sad there'll be no more teenage anythings

1705 cleaning my paint brush using methylated spirits

1706 daubing an itch with turpentine

1707 six of one or half-a-dozen of the other

1708 when the people in the next apartment transfer *their* junk mail into *our* letterbox, even though we have a sticker on ours which says 'NO JUNK MAIL'

1709 I transfer our neighbours' junk mail back from *our* letterbox into *their* letterbox — hoping it was theirs in the first place — to teach them a lesson (hoping I got it right)

1710 mum-shaming

1711 dad-shaming

1712 baby-shaming

1713 any and all forms of political correctness

1714 politicians with red hair who flip-flop over bills before the Senate

1715 politicians who see things only as black or white

1716 when I have car problems

1717 like yesterday when the electronic key wouldn't unlock the car (everything was dead) and, because I was stranded, I called roadside assistance, who sent a guy within the hour

1718 and the roadside assistance guy was a clever thief who broke into the car using wire

1719 and he got the car going

1720 but then the car's air-conditioning blew up

1721 and then this morning — hoping to get the air con fixed — the car wouldn't start, again

1722 so again I called the roadside assistance people, who sent a battery guy within the hour

1723 but the battery guy they sent wasn't a trained thief, and he couldn't break into the car

1724 so he called his office and asked them to send a mechanic guy, who was a trained thief

1725 and the guy who came was the same mechanic from yesterday, the same trained thief

1726 and again he broke into the car using the same wire as yesterday

1727 and he got the car going, like he did yesterday

1728 and he told me to take the car to the battery place where I'd recently got a new battery

1729 but the battery guy told me to take the car to the auto-electrical guy around the corner

1730 and the auto-electrical guy told me to leave the car with him for two days

1731 and then I had to walk home — and was stressed by where all of this was leading

1732 and how, the next day, the auto-electrical guy called to say it will cost $750 to repair

1733 and how I sat on a chair, and wept

1734 the 'K' in Kmart is the first letter of its founder's name (don't ask me who)

1735 when we had a farm, it was 47 acres; but using metrics, we had only 19 hectares

1736 I've discovered I can get a new pen at penisland.net

1737 *give me a classified departmental briefing and I will decide which 'medevacked' refugees will stay and who among them will be sent back to Manis Island and Nauru*

1738 the Uber GPS wants us to go to the local shops via Brisbane; the driver is clueless

1739 when you have to say to the Uber driver, *'Next left'*, *'Next right'*, *'Next left'*

1740 when a taxi driver sees you are about to get into an Uber — and he yells abuse at you

1741 whatever happened to The Pentagon Papers?

1742 whatever happened to the cost of lamb?

1743 how come no one on TV ever has to go to the toilet?

1744 there have been 137 commonwealth royal commissions since 1902

1745 people who conceal evidence

1746 people who doctor evidence

1747 people who manufacture evidence

1748 skulduggerous types who conceal, doctor and manufacture evidence

1749 saline injections and sugar pills given to complaining hypochondriacs, to shut them up

1750 each day, 700 Australians retire and begin to draw down on their superannuation fund

1751 each week, retirees withdraw $140 billion from their superannuation fund

1752 I withdraw $459 per fortnight from my superannuation fund

1753 I pay $9 per fortnight for the privilege of withdrawing $459 from my super fund

1754 I think I'm on top of things

1755 people who complain are to write their complaints neatly on a sheet of paper, place the sheet of paper in a nice envelope, and then burn the envelope — because no one gives a ...

1756 again this year our Council rates notice offers two options for paying the rates: in four or ten instalments; again no mention of the *third* option: paying the whole amount up front

1757 when my younger son Jamie was alive, I would tell him a particular problem I was facing, and he'd say, '*Call the RACV — They Care!*'

1758 when Jamie was alive and he would hang all kinds of shit on me

1759 when Jamie was thirteen, he made a quarter-size table tennis table (with quarter-size net), great for small spaces. He called it 'Plong' (play on ping pong). I took his design to Taiwan and had a real version made, but, when I brought it home, folk at Target said the economics didn't stack up; Jamie's clever invention came to naught (or I was just a hopeless salesman)

1760 clever inventions which come to naught (especially ones made by a thirteen-year-old)

1761 government and government-funded bodies which say they 'donate' money to charitable causes; they do not *donate* funds; they *'allocate'*. Donating refers to philanthropy — and government officials certainly don't donate *their* money; they give away *ours*

1762 energy providers no longer use the ugly term 'blackout'; they now call it 'load shedding' or 'brown-outing'

1763 curiouser and curiouser

1764 sugar and spice

1765 all things nice

1766 sexarche

1767 aged care royal commission: 'staff caught betting on which patients will die next'

1768 agricultural college chair: *'The best committee is two with the second bloke sick'*

1769 Bhutan and UAE have government ministries for happiness; can you imagine that happening in Australia?

1770 news report: 'Australian high school students record the lowest ever scores in reading, maths and science'

1771 the young woman on the tram who didn't stand for me was reading a book on resilience; I hope the next book she reads will be one on manners

1772 it's 'should have', not 'should of'

1773 how corrupt is the TV ad where a jockey gives betting advice to a group of millennials

1774 news item: 'Chinese MP linked to cash drop'; surely, no, that can't possibly be true!

1775 henceforth, I wish to be referred to as **Sir Michael Thornton** (it has a nice ring to it)

1776 bemused is not amused; it is bewildered or perplexed

1777 a 'high-roller' places $1 million bets; I play a 2c machine with a $10 session limit

1778 founder means establish; flounder is to stagger clumsily, or a fish

1779 Santa has been reading posts on Facebook; most people will be getting a dictionary

1780 tears are the lubricant of the soul

1781 sign on store window: 'Trading Hours: When We Feel Like Opening, We Will'

1782 a friend said that each morning I should list three things of gratitude; today's are (1) I woke up, (2) I have the whole day to be pissed off, (3) tonight I can go back to bed

1783 I put out a call on Facebook asking friends to tell me things which piss them off, but no one replied — and that pissed me right off

1784 children in war-torn countries who leave school on Friday afternoon and don't eat again until they return to school on Monday morning

1785 poverty

1786 disadvantage

1787 malnutrition

1788 impoverishment

1789 neediness

1790 necessitousness

1791 Australia's foreign aid budget has been reduced in each of the past six years and is now at an all-time low, at 21 cents in every $100 of national government expenditure

1792 Twenty-five Australians have been killed by crocodile attacks in the past fifty years

1793 Forty-seven Australians have been killed by shark attacks in the past fifty years

1794 bogans who bash a poker machine, thinking it will land winning symbols for them

1795 there are 390 million guns in America, owned by just 22% of the population

1796 bogans

1797 idiots

1798 bogans who are idiots

1799 why don't coffee vans drive around suburbs like ice-cream vans once did?

1800 people who think they are clever and important, but don't actually *create* anything

1801 TV news services which distort the faces of evildoers as they're led to a police van

1802 people who post on Facebook that they're at an airport; jaw-dropping news

1803 the old dear on the scooter in the Optus ad who has plenty of time to avoid crashing into the table at which four other oldies are sitting, petrified of the pending calamity

1804 your smart TV is watching you constantly, reporting to someone what you're doing

1805 when we fly to Manila, to avoid getting deep vein thrombosis, every hour I climb over passengers and pace the aisle for 10 minutes, then climb back over the same people

1806 Whitney no longer will always love me

1807 Elvis no longer will know what wise men say

1808 Freddie no longer will thank us all

1809 Buddy never again will feel it raining in his heart

1810 I no longer walk on certain streets for fear of a huge building or crane falling on me

1811 when the waiter says they're out of the item I've meticulously chosen from the menu

1812 my friend and his grandson were standing on their yacht; my friend asked the lad to toss him his keys — and the replacement electronic car key dooverlackie cost $780

1813 being *obsessed* with solving the nine-letter-word in the newspaper, I've developed a habit of searching everywhere for nine-letter-words. Such as when I take my daughter to the eye hospital, I look for signs and notices for nine-letter-words; words like ambulance, reception, inpatient, infection, trembling, frightful, scariness, mortality, irregular, pneumonia, startling, blindness, injection, flippitty, orphanage, crocodile, brainless, addiction, suffering, conscious, whizzbang

1814 yet another huge crane buckles in Melbourne's CBD

1815 for people who don't know what a dooverlackie is, it's a watchamacallit

1816 for people who don't know what a watchamacallit is, it's a thingummyjig

1817 for people who don't know what a thingummyjig is, it's what unlocks the car door

1818 I'm not sure if the plant food is doing much good out there on the balcony plants

1819 the formal sex education I was supposed to receive at boarding school didn't happen

1820 the informal sex education I wasn't supposed to receive at boarding school did happen

1821 when the lethal drain clearing liquid isn't quite lethal enough

1822 pomp and ceremony

1823 to the best of my knowledge and understanding I've not been trolled

1824 not having the slightest clue what it means to be trolled

1825 things are crook when the only way to satisfy a travel urge is by watching 'Getaway'

1826 having a detective for a daughter-in-law is a huge comfort

1827 worried the car service centre would rip me off, but all I needed was new mirror fluid

1828 no way in the Woolworths ad is the girl carrying a *full* box of cherries — it's fake

1829 only thirteen days until pension day

1830 loud people

1831 people with severe body odour

1832 people with severe body odour and who are loud

1833 my oh my gosh! A supermarket passes on to dairy farmers *only* 3.5 cents of a 10-cent levy designed purposely to help struggling dairy farmers

1834 unsung heroes

1835 Australia Day honours given to people for doing their paid job — the higher their salary, it seems the higher the award

1836 lamb's fry and bacon at my local — at a pensioner discount price

1837 when you do someone a favour and they don't reciprocate or thank you

1838 our Christmas decorations might look pathetic, but it's the thought that counts

1839 (six hours later) Kass arrives home and says the Christmas decorations are pathetic

1840 (six hours later) Kass has redesigned our Christmas decorations — beautifully

1841 one's life might be humdrum, but it's the cheap beer at happy hour which counts

1842 Wednesday supper with Denis, Darren and Andrew at 1; eye test at 2; chiropractor at 3; car service at 4; happy hour at the pub at 5; nap at 6; bed at 7; day complete

1843 politicians who make mean and callous laws, then cry for the cameras

1844 the worst possible time to have a heart attack is during a game of charades

1845 when you've forgotten to buy new dish washing liquid

1846 being too lazy to write a shopping list and consequently buying all the wrong stuff

1847 as always, I forgot to take a plastic bag, which means I had to buy yet another one

1848 *'Never complain and never explain'* — Kerry Packer

1849 *'Why are people so unkind?'* — Kamahl

1850 *'The best way to help the poor is to not become one'* — Lang Hancock

1851 *'All our best heroes are losers'* — Richard Glover

1852 *'Shoot straight, you bastards'* — Breaker Morant

1853 *'Such is life'* — Ned Kelly

1854 *'Some mistakes are too much fun to make only once'* — anon

1855 *'A mistake made once is okay; the same mistake made twice makes you an idiot'* — me

1856 the distance between your ear lobes and the distance between your nipples is the same

1857 global warming

1858 a problem is a potential solution

1859 French agitators pushing for the age pension to start at age fifty

1860 sign on my *chiropractor's* door: *'Consultations now available by video'* (apparently, my chiropractor shares his consulting room with one of the GPs in their practice)

1861 regardless, I told my chiropractor — and this because he always hurts me — that from now on I want all of my consultations with him to be via video (try cracking my back, eh?)

1862 a notice in the doctors' waiting room: 'Please let

us know that you've arrived' (I guess if you haven't yet arrived, you don't need to let them know)

1863 for the life of me I cannot get my head around rugby — and I've tried *so* hard

1864 I still believe the royalty payment I receive annually from the government for copies of my book borrowed from public libraries is too good a thing to last

1865 and so the auto electrician guy fixed the electricals

1866 and I paid him the $750

1867 but the air con still didn't work

1868 so I took the car to my service guy

1869 and he said to come back Monday

1870 so I did

1871 and he fixed it

1872 and he charged me $220 to fix it

1873 if only I knew then what I know now

1874 people who change channels without asking

1875 when Australia runs out of milk (and dairy farmers), it's then that I plan to speak up

1876 life can be such a bitch

1877 back when I worked in school fundraising, Chinese parents wanting to enrol their child would say, *'We give money!'*; then, after the child got in, I would say, *'Now may we talk about voluntary giving?'*; to which I'd receive a *'Solly, we no speak English'*

1878 when the smoke alarm goes off because I've overcooked the pork belly

1879 when the smoke alarm won't stop barking despite frantically waving a tea towel at it

1880 continually being asked to take an after-sale survey, starting with, *'How did we do?'*

1881 when I told my children I'd revised my will, and they asked how I was feeling

1882 having to continually tell websites that I'm not a robot

1883 the impossibility of having a doggy door onto our balcony because the walls are all-glass

1884 the cost of putting a doggy into boarding kennels during holidays

1885 the staggering cost of taking a doggy to a vet

1886 knowing who would take a doggy on its twice-daily walks — and pick up its poo

1887 not wanting to argue about the total impossibility of having a doggy

1888 the final edition for the year of ABC TV 'Insiders' and, of all the people they could have chosen to interview, they chose Mathias Cormann

1889 'Not at Chemist Warehouse, it's not!'

1890 the bogan dumb-arse at the Macca's drive-through who orders one of everything

1891 my mind keeps returning to my *two* big breakdowns after Jamie died

1892 despite all of my many blessings, my mind fears another breakdown could happen

1893 employing numerous mindfulness strategies to stave off another breakdown

1894 Australia was just the second country in the world to give women the vote

1895 someone please let me in on their ultra-lucrative scam — strictly for research purposes

1896 typos in manuscripts

1897 typos in published works

1898 mistakes

1899 errors

1900 botch-ups

1901 blunders

1902 clangers

1903 my New Year's resolution is to give up all my addictions, other than this one

1904 ditto my next one, and the one after that

1905 no, Channel 7, people do not put up festive lights; they put up Christmas lights

1906 amazing how on Twitter normally polite professional commentators become seriously vile and vulgar

1907 whatever happened to men's baggy, corduroy trousers?

1908 watching golf for truly rotten shots and awful lies (like watching car racing for prangs)

1909 Prince Charles's Aston Martin is one car I *won't* be adding to my vintage car collection

1910 a face lift is the last thing I want in life (or after it)

1911 the prime minister has done it again; '... *to Jenny and I*'

1912 wanting to tell your family at Christmas that you love them, but why does it have to cost money?

1913 politician announces her retirement with lots of media splash

1914 she says she hopes to secure a senior position in the not-for-profit sector

1915 how many kids on $14 an hour would love to get such free publicity to promote their career aspirations?

1916 I swear the girl sitting next to me on the shopping centre's courtesy seating, breast-feeding her tiny infant, was not a day older than fifteen

1917 living with erectile disfunction can be hard

1918 yoghurt kiosks are a total rip-off

1919 the secret to the yoghurt kiosk is to have a tiny taste — *not* to fill the cup to the brim

1920 they say Chadstone will soon join up with Crown casino

1921 I say close down each and every toy shop which sells guns — fake or otherwise

1922 long queues of under-thirties queuing to enter boutique fashion shops, all texting

1923 beauty and innocence are wasted on youth

1924 they say what's in a shopping trolley tells you everything about a person

1925 so, why did the granny have a big pack of tampons in her shopping trolley?

1926 'Meet you at The Reject Shop'

1927 god-botherers

1928 to calculate the diameter of a circle, multiply the radius by 2. If you don't have the radius, divide the circumference of the circle by π to get the diameter. If you don't have the radius or the circumference, divide the area of the circle by π and then find that number's square root to get the radius. If you don't have the radius, circumference or diameter, you're stuffed

1929 it's 57 years since I was in year 9; how on earth am I expected to remember π?

1930 car ads which boast a 4.9% interest rate when the official interest rate is 0.25%

1931 the beauty of SBS 'Child Genius' is that the kids haven't yet learnt to be horrible

1932 SBS 'Child Genius' claims boys inherit their intelligence from their mother; hmm!

1933 my mother, who played at Wimbledon in 1939, used to say her brains were in her feet

1934 I'm sure Virginia Trioli said casting 'nasturtiums' (a flower) instead of aspersions

1935 whatever became of Rhonda and Ketut?

1936 milk sells for less than water — how can a developed country allow this to be?

1937 the margin of error granted by speed cameras is 3 km/hr

1938 my heart urges me to apply to go on 'Mastermind'; my mind tells me I'm an imbecile

1939 the government says we should limit per capita water usage to 155 litres per day

1940 tell that to Kass

1941 when I step into a train looking forward to a peaceful journey to the City, and there is half a primary school in *my* carriage, it's time to wait a day

1942 shopping centre Santa is replaced by a Sustainability Pirate; WHAT?

1943 the number of men who pull up at the bus stop and ask my daughter if she's available

1944 I've 'unsubscribed' from my last remaining work-related email notification; hooray!

1945 how it pisses me off when I lapse into a happy state of mind — when I don't deserve to

1946 Rebel Wilson has had enough exposure already

1947 the stupid ad where a guy puts his car out with other people's hard rubbish — when he could have got $2,000 as a *minimum* trade-in for it

1948 two guys on 'The Project' promote their book on the demise of creativity — when Sir Ken Robinson gave a brilliant Ted Talk on the exact same thing *fifteen years ago*

1949 a so-called work of art — a banana stuck to a wall with duct tape — sells for $175,000

1950 a protester eats the banana

1951 push comes to shove, eventually

1952 you plan your shopping outing exactly — but when you get there the shop is gone

1953 how millions of moronic evangelicals thought Trump is 'the chosen one'

1954 when I've missed a meeting

1955 my head is shaved but still I fancy having a bun

1956 my blind, single-parent, diabetic daughter with dreadful teeth rang a talkback radio station on the topic of bad teeth — and a dentist gave her a free $30,000 mouth makeover

1957 people who answer a question with a question

1958 swimming pools with green water

1959 swimming pools with no water

1960 news report: 'Australia sells water rights to foreign interests for $490m'; OUR water

1961 academic calls for the world to give up on the use of apostrophes'

1962 the number of Mercedes drivers who, frankly, cannot drive a car to save themselves

1963 how such incompetent Mercedes drivers have enough smarts to afford a Mercedes

1964 next year's *Time* person-of-the-year will be a 16-year-old private school boy from Point Piper on his 'Ls,' who already has a Ferrari in the garage but can't see the garage due to Sydney's air pollution, and who thinks climate change is a conspiracy

1965 I thought the big guy at *my* café was a super-rich businessman, but he's a retired cop

1966 the trouble with assuming things

1967 slow wi-fi

1968 no wi-fi

1969 when I forget the wi-fi password seconds after the hotel receptionist tells me it

1970 Geeks-To-You make it all sound *so* easy

1971 saying 'investors' when you mean 'greedy, inhumane, ruthless, selfish pricks'

1972 footballers who eat *a whole row* of Weet-Bix in one sitting

1973 it's bedtime but I can't sleep — the radio talkback is too interesting to turn off

1974 bed linen which is smelly, has dribble stains, and is much overdue for the laundry

1975 people who delight in endlessly popping bubble-wrap as noisily as they can

1976 the Indian granny on the bus who thought I wanted to listen to her ghastly music

1977 the tiger snake which used to perch in the tree by our kitchen door

1978 the thought of living in a place where I'd need to shovel snow to go anywhere

1979 beards

1980 when I plan a family fun day out — and Kass hates it

1981 *'Didn't we have a lovely time the day we went to Bangor?'*

1982 people who define personal disasters as 'character building', as in *'Their house burned down and the dog died, and the neighbour described it as character building'*

1983 next time, I want to come back as Tiger Woods

1984 Tiger Woods's career earnings are estimated at US$1.5b, his net worth about US$800m

1985 hotels which display cheap plastic sachets of breakfast foods instead of open bowlfuls

1986 let Scotland secede

1987 let Western Australia secede

1988 let everyone succeed

1989 swimmers who ignore the red flags — and expect lifeguards to rescue them, as a right

1990 one-time US presidential candidate Ross Perot who, in 1979, passed on an opportunity to buy Microsoft for US$60 million

1991 Blockbuster, which, in 2000, passed on buying Netflix for US$50 million

1992 *twelve* publishing houses passed on publishing JK Rowling's first Harry Potter book before Bloomsbury took it on after the MD's 9-year-old daughter persuaded her dad

1993 kits and caboodles

1994 I was once told that mayonnaise is one molecule shy of paint

1995 Aussie Feliks Zemdegs, 22, set a world record for solving a Rubik's Cube — *4.22 secs*

1996 in 2008, Adelaide woman Irene O'Shea became the world's oldest skydiver at the age of 102 years and 193 days — it wasn't reported if she broke anything upon landing

1997 Perth holds the record for having the world's tallest blow-up water slide — 22.4m

1998 when my watch stops and I need to know the time — and I'm too stupid to think of looking at the great big clock on my phone

1999 when my watch stops and the band breaks, and my phone runs out of oomph

2000 sugar in coffee

2001 sugar in tea

2002 sugar

2003 uneven footpaths

2004 recliner furniture, which is reluctant to recline

2005 the number of women who do sex work solely to pay their kids' private school fees

2006 Victoria has eighty-eight licensed brothels

2007 when delicious but ridiculously expensive cheese is way beyond my budget

2008 being pestered by waiters

2009 being pestered by real estate agents

2010 being pestered by energy companies

2011 whatever happened to *'Cheerio?'*

2012 two mobile phones, one charger

2013 points *taken* from junior sporting teams if they win by too much

2014 our body corporate charge has just gone up by 12% (inflation is 1.9%)

2015 wondering if the token nativity scene at our local mall is due to tightness of the billionaire mall owners, or more to do with political correctness; either way, it's pathetic

2016 travelling all the way to Nepal just to stare at Mt Everest

2017 the contestant on Mastermind who didn't know that the fifth borough of New York City is Staten Island (surely everyone knows that)

2018 Victoria legislates mandatory jail for violence towards emergency workers; soon after, a 22-year-old avoids jail *twice* for punching and headbutting an emergency worker

2019 news report: 'Media baron buys Californian house for $217m' — the amount needed to employ 217 journalists, or 542 cadet journalists, for 10 years

2020 why are the recommended serving portions of ham always so pathetically small?

2021 copious advice on the Internet on how to discipline a recalcitrant child — when a good hard smack will do the trick every time

2022 I know. Let's turn a few overseas multi-millionaires into billionaires by letting them buy and sell water misappropriated from struggling, drought-affected Aussie farmers

2023 having to suffer 7 whole minutes and 20 whole seconds of 'MacArthur Park'

2024 I'm blowed if I can get a mango to prolapse successfully

2025 funny money

2026 spoiled for choice

2027 *'That's the way.'*

2028 how, when we had a farm, I stupidly used to throw glyphosate ('Roundup') around with gay abandon (I should be dead already)

2029 it's time to sniff the wind on climate change, PM; you'll find 51% of the electorate wants immediate action; time to imitate coach John Kennedy and *'DO SOMETHING!'*

2030 as I grow older, my Christmas shopping list gets shorter because the things I want to give as gifts, to those I love, can't be bought

2031 Talkeetna in Alaska once had, as its mayor, a cat called Stubbs

2032 toilet paper in France is predominantly pink

2033 Viagra, when dissolved in water, will keep a plant alive and erect for an extra week

2034 the utter rudeness of being given a gift card to a fitness centre

2035 in 2004, a missing woman was found among the search party looking for her

2036 overseas banks have psychologists to help filthy rich clients cope with their wealth

2037 award winning vanilla slices at Bayswater

2038 award winning vanilla slices at Mansfield

2039 award winning vanilla slices at Ouyen

2040 excursions currently being planned to Bayswater, Mansfield and Ouyen

2041 Q. *'Do you always sleep in the nude?'* A. *'What does it look like?'*

2042 India buys Aussie cricketer for $3.1m; think what that sum could do for India's poor

2043 on second thoughts, I wish to come back as James Blunt — singing requires less walking than golf (were I instead to come back as Tiger Woods)

2044 I declare James Blunt the winner over David Archeleta, Calum Scott and Ed Sheeran

2045 except when James sings *'Sacrifice'* in concert with Ed Sheeran, then they're equal

2046 James singing *'Goodbye My Lover'* at Oxford University

2047 the lousy, talentless audience member at the Oxford concert who didn't applaud James

2048 damn it, I totally missed the recent James Blunt concert at Rochford Winery

2049 I've just discovered Andrea and Matteo Bocelli singing *'Perfect'* on YouTube

2050 a tomato has fallen off the balcony vine — I'm pissed, given the water I've fed it

2051 it's time to reconnoitre all of the things which piss me off; the list is like endless

2052 if you sneeze while driving at 100 km/hr, your eyes will shut for 47 metres

2053 experts say you are three times more likely to get a computer virus from a religious website than from a porn website (good, I'm safe; phew!)

2054 bookstore browsers are 3.5 times more likely to buy a book on romance if the shop smells of chocolate

2055 hairs in my ears and nose

2056 there are old men in Hanoi who remove nose and ear hair at their roadside stall

2057 more than 500,000 Australian adults identify as gay

2058 Australia is the world's fifth most gay-friendly country, behind Spain, Germany, Canada and the Czech Republic

2059 shopping centres which play classical music in the car park to repel teenage hooligans

2060 for goodness sake, the name is Michael, *not* Mick or Mikey or Micheal

2061 I've found the 'Settings' button on my smart phone — and now my phone rings *me*

2062 I can't find the shop which sells old-man's braces (for my trousers, not my teeth)

2063 you know what? I don't care that I'm getting old, because the way the world is headed, I, like most baby boomers, don't want to be around to see mother earth implode

2064 New South Wales has an underground coal fire which has been burning for 5,500 years

2065 an enterprising Aussie tried to sell New Zealand on eBay

2066 two US teens traded on eBay; they started with a paper clip and ended with a house

2067 the average drink-driver drives over the limit *eighty times* before getting caught

2068 seven-dollar movie tickets for sessions prior to midday — now that's good value

2069 I couldn't care less that I'm no longer allowed to climb Uluru

2070 I'm an odd number. Take away one letter in my name and I become even. I am …?

2071 pissed I missed the 3-hour 'Messiah', which Handel wrote in 18 days, in 1742

2072 George Burns: *'My doctor told me to give up smoking. Doctor's dead.'*

2073 Bob Hope: *'You know you're getting old when the candles cost more than the cake'*

2074 Lucille Ball: *'The secret to staying young is to live honestly, eat slowly, and lie about your age'*

2075 Jack Benny: *'Age is about mind over matter. I don't mind, and you don't matter'*

2076 Archie Bunker: 'Patience is a virgin'

2077 Tommy Cooper: 'Last night I dreamed I ate a marshmallow. When I woke up the pillow was gone'

2078 Tommy Cooper: 'A doctor told a woman her bad back was due to old age. The woman said she wanted a second opinion, so he said, "Okay, you're ugly, as well."'

2079 eating 90 grams of polar bear liver can kill you

2080 'Do yellow balls go further?' — TV golf commentator

2081 I need to let you in on a secret: the previous decade did NOT end on 31.12.19; it ended on 31.12.20. (AD began on 01.01.00) How can people be *so* stupid?

2082 it's nap time, again (to replenish the brain fuel needed to continue compiling this list)

2083 each sheep which grazes on a station on the Nullarbor Plain requires *240 times* more land area to survive than a sheep which grazes on valuable pasture in western Victoria

2084 on average, people live for three years after they make a will (so don't make one!)

2085 each week seventy visitors to Australia overstay their tourist visa

2086 only one in five people wash their hands after going to the toilet

2087 one-third of adults sleep with a fluffy toy (other than a human fluffy toy)

2088 telling American friends to wear thongs to the beach is likely to unsettle them

2089 the Eiffel Tower grows by six inches in the Paris midsummer heat

2090 because English pigeon poo has gunpowder-making properties, the Queen owns it

2091 my grandfather was appointed an honorary policeman during the 1923 police strike

2092 hares are born with fur and sight; rabbits are born naked and blind

2093 in 2012, an Afghan Taliban commander handed himself in, demanding he be given the $100 reward he'd seen for himself on a poster

2094 almost is the longest English word with all of its letters in alphabetical order

2095 surgeons who play video games at least 3 hours a week perform their day job 27% faster and make 37% fewer mistakes

2096 a letter writer to a newspaper tells a columnist to 'HAPPY UP'

2097 if a reader dares to tell me to 'HAPPY UP', I will fart in his face

2098 happy for people who win 'Hard Quiz' or 'Hot Seat' or 'Mastermind' or 'The Chase'

2099 the world's biggest pineapple, at 32 cm and 8.29 kg, was grown at Bakewell, 25 km south of Darwin

2100 when you've gotta go, you've gotta go

2101 e is the most commonly-used letter in the alphabet — it appears in 11% of all words

2102 baked beans are stewed, not baked

2103 companies rename Christmas to be 'inclusive floating cultural holidays'; WHAT?

2104 Hawaii's flag includes the Union Jack (we think *we've* got problems)

2105 I tried to binge on Nutella, but nuts got in the way

2106 the button said, *'Press for customer service'*, so I did, and the man serving abused me

2107 who, in today's mad, unrelenting, chaotic world has the time or patience to shell peas?

2108 cheap, watery yoghurt with bland and soggy 'seconds' fruit

2109 in Ohio, convicted drunk drivers must drive with different coloured number plates

2110 I am yet to visit 9,971 of Australia's 10,000 beaches

2111 how much of Australia needs to burn (and lives so sadly be lost) before authorities agree that climate change is present, real and undeniable — and requires ACTION?

2112 the USA has conducted over 1,000 nuclear weapon tests; France, over 200

2113 women were first allowed to run in the Boston Marathon in 1972

2114 willy-nilly

2115 at a time when betting and gambling is so on-the-nose, the AFL signs an $8 million deal with a betting agency — they are so incredibly good at gauging public sentiment; not

2116 we use twelve muscles to smile and eleven to frown

2117 the archbishop of Orlando is archbishop of the moon; can't get into much strife there

2118 of course it's the father who's portrayed as the dumb-arse idiot in the El-Maco ad

2119 Kass: *'Do you want to see the new Star Wars movie?'* Me: *'I need to see the dentist'*

2120 asking how the world allowed China to build a military base in international waters?

2121 fireworks and formula one racing take equal first prize for being the world's greatest mis-use of public money

2122 I was going to say Australia doesn't have concentration camps, like China, but we do!

2123 six million millennials are going to have to pay for us five million baby boomers

2124 serves the millennials right; the entitled, lazy blighters they are (my children excepted)

2125 got it; elect me and we'll have a Ministry for Empathy, Love and Happiness

2126 President Joe Biden: *'Failure at some point in your life is inevitable, but giving up is unforgivable'*

2127 twenty-one of the 135 boys in my school year group (16%) are no longer alive

2128 people shouldn't have to turn to a TV current affairs show to get justice

2129 I thought TV stations were no longer going to post betting odds during matches

2130 so pleased Tennis Australia has not succumbed to betting adverts at the Open

2131 is it Sandpapergate or people having less money that's causing poor cricket crowds?

2132 I've never known the answer to one single question posed by the *Herald Sun*'s Jon Anderson on 3AW's breakfast show each weekday; his sporting knowledge is amazing

2133 I didn't believe the megastore salesman who said he could give me *only* fifty dollars off because he'd be left with only a $15 margin — and the store's owner is a mega-billionaire

2134 notwithstanding the glamour and glitz projected in its media advertising, over 10,000 people are banned from entering Crown Casino; some glitz, some glamour

2135 Churchill: *'Hitler said he'd wring my neck like a chicken; some neck, some chicken'*

2136 happy to have New Zealand's beautiful national anthem over our dirge any time

2137 (controversial:) I reckon musical theatre has stuck to the same formula for too long

2138 Caltex reportedly changing its name to Ampol — it makes me feel seventeen again

2139 generally speaking, songs are becoming increasingly bland (bring back The Beatles)

2140 in the 1930s, the government declared war on emus; 2,500 rounds of ammunition were hurled at the emus but not one emu was killed

2141 how come when I fill the car, and I stop at an exact amount (say $55), then, while I'm putting the hose back on its hook, the metre clicks over to $55.01; *every time*

2142 'Your paper sucks' (letter to the editor)

2143 'I hate you' (letter to the editor)

2144 'Man-hater seeks man to hate' (advertisement in the 'personals' column)

2145 belly dancing with a colostomy bag

2146 'We know there are known knowns; there are things we know we know. We also know there are known unknowns; that is to say we know there are things we do not know'

2147 doing a Donald Rumsfeld

2148 news report: 'Panda mating fails: vet takes over'

2149 news report: 'Criminals get nine months in violin case'

2150 news report: 'Children make nutritious snacks'

2151 $71 million up for grabs at the 2020 Australian Open tennis; more unjustifiable absurdity when those companies could spend their money to make society more equitable

2152 would someone please tell Apple that here in Australia we don't say 'Happy holidays'; we say *'Happy Christmas'* — and proudly so. Get it? Got it? Good!

2153 English funnyman Les Dawson took his wife to southern Spain on a holiday; he said how at the beach his wife bent over to pick up her sunglasses — and Gibraltar had an eclipse

2154 the early bird might get the worm — but the second mouse gets the cheese

2155 I intend to live forever; so far, so good

2156 the PM — 'ScottyFromMarketing' — is so good at spin, he can tell you to go to hell in a way that makes you look forward to the trip

2157 if the world didn't suck, we'd all fall off

2158 where there's a will there's a litigious relative

2159 mean and nasty people who make crude, rude and hurtful jokes

2160 like you know you're a bogan if you can like name every driver at like Bathurst

2161 like if there are more than like seven McDonald's hamburger wrappers in your like car

2162 like if you mow your grass and you like find a car like underneath

2163 think of the poor dolts who spend all of Christmas Day changing price labels in shops

2164 from where in goodness name did *'Give it up for'* come? (a round of applause, please)

2165 in 2016, 80% of white evangelicals voted for Trump (the other 20% were women)

2166 in late 2019, US magazine *Christianity Today* published an editorial describing Trump as 'immoral', and called for his removal

2167 the following week the magazine lost 2,000 subscribers, but picked up 5,000 new ones

2168 remember the y2k bug scare? (just who made all of the money out of that one?)

2169 Dr Google says I can expect to live another 14 years

2170 at seventy-one, I'm considered to be 'middle old' (as opposed to 'young old' or 'very old')

2171 writers are told they need to find their 'voice'; I've looked everywhere for mine

2172 show, don't tell

2173 Melbourne's New Year's Eve fireworks, including security, cost $4 million

2174 why would you have a box of salad home delivered when you can make up your own plate for one-tenth of the cost?

2175 the *average* Barcelona soccer salary is *twelve million dollars*

2176 people who stand still on the right side of an escalator

2177 people who want to walk up the left side of an escalator

2178 cyclists in my lane

2179 people who call a shopping trolley a shopping cart

2180 people who talk with their hands

2181 people who lick their knife

2182 people who crack their knuckles

2183 people who click their pen

2184 people who tap their feet

2185 people who leave lights on

2186 people who died at seventy: King George V, Howard Hughes, Orson Wells, Marco Polo, Louis Vuitton, Niki Lauda, Rudyard Kipling, James Earl Ray, Buster Keaton, Nina Simone, Joe Cocker, Hans Christian Andersen, Euclid, Allen Ginsberg, Kim Jong-il, Nelson Rockefeller, Roddy McDowall, Annette Funicello, Henry Mancini — yikes!

2187 people in the supermarket who change their mind and dump an item on a foreign shelf

2188 people who don't RSVP, because they're hoping a better offer will come along

2189 beaten by Kass at 10-pin bowling — and it was the first time she'd played

2190 the person who was asked by a *very* prominent Australian to be best man at the latter's wedding and is still wondering why he was asked

2191 keenly anticipating Danube River cruise tickets from Santa

2192 *'Fully Paid-Up and Proud Hawks Member'* sticker on a car in the staff car park of a local hotel owned by the Carlton Football Club

2193 *'Go Pies'* sticker on another car in the same Carlton-owned hotel car park

2194 passengers sitting behind me on a plane who continually *kick* and *pull* on the back of my seat, especially when they leave their seat to go to the toilet

2195 well before he became prime minister, John Curtin was jailed for three days for failing to comply with a compulsory medical exam for conscription

2196 before he became a senator, Derryn Hinch was jailed three times for contempt of court and breaching suppression orders (for dutifully disclosing the whereabouts of paedophiles)

2197 after she'd been a parliamentarian (the first time), Pauline Hanson was ordered to serve three years jail for bribery and fraud, but was later acquitted

2198 I went to school with the son of the chap who invented the *tap* in the wine cask

2199 through a previous marriage, I was related to the man who invented the black box

2200 in 1889, Aussie Arthur James Arnot invented the electric drill

2201 in 1978, Aussie Professor Graeme Clark invented the Cochlear ear implant

2202 in 1993, Aussie Jim Frazier invented the deep focus camera lens

2203 in 1998, the Reserve Bank of Australia, CSIRO and the University of Melbourne jointly invented the Polymer bank note, which now is used in twenty-nine countries

2204 in 1999, Western Australia's Professor Fiona Wood invented the spray-on skin technique

2205 in 2006, Aussie Professor Ian Frazer invented vaccines for cervical cancer

2206 okay, I give up on 'gotten'; and I've definitely given up on 'cool'

2207 what's this about calling sporting teams *franchises*?

2208 people who crave recognition, fame and fortune

2209 people who queue overnight for Boxing Day sales and tickets to the football finals

2210 the sadness which is the demise of Hong Kong as we once knew and loved it

2211 Carrie Lam

2212 the sadness which is Myanmar today

2213 Aung San Suu Kyi

2214 the best way to get conservatives to accept climate change is to show them how to make millions of dollars out of it

2215 falling from grace

2216 I'm ready for tomorrow's nine-letter-word puzzle in *The Age* because I've learned bumfuzzle, kabeljouw, hypoxemic, whichaway, kibbutzim, monkeypox and vowelised

2217 government subsidies for sport and media and all other forms of misappropriation

2218 people who do super-dangerous things and then require taxpayers to rescue them

2219 that there aren't more all-women crews in the Melbourne to Hobart yacht race

2220 governments which refuse to come clean and admit that the placement of speed cameras is for road safety purposes *but also* to boost 'budgeted' government revenue

2221 the former talkback host, now senator, who dumped a caller wanting to plug a charity

2222 *Five thousand* babies are rescued from locked cars in shopping centre car parks each year

2223 for Christmas lunch, an aged care facility served

residents baked beans with two dollops of mashed potato — while the facility owner had turkey, ham, and all the trimmings

2224 when life becomes topsy-turvy

2225 millennials who don't 'touch-on' on the tram, notice me watching them, and smirk

2226 millennials who don't 'touch-on' and roll their eyes at old people, like me, who do

2227 some people bring happiness wherever they go, others bring happiness *whenever* they go

2228 the two scruffy-looking men who drove past me with *two* parking tickets on their windscreen

2229 when a film is herky-jerky

2230 when my car becomes herky-jerky

2231 when life becomes herky-jerky

2232 Churchill's cigar, Roosevelt's cigarettes and Stalin's pipe

2233 turn it up

2234 greeting: 'I thought you were dead'

2235 greeting: 'I didn't recognise you with your clothes on'

2236 greeting: 'Was it you to whom I once was married?'

2237 my late headmaster's autobiography is called *Richly Rewarding*

2238 I wish my schooldays had been richly rewarding

2239 the Lexus ad is suspect because, after all, who could afford a Lexus *and* eat cherries?

2240 still looking at our dishwasher and wondering how it works

2241 me to waiter: *'When I said mains later, I didn't mean tomorrow'*

2242 the waiter who decided to fill the straw dispenser and wipe down a few tables before getting me the beer I requested

2243 something seriously is out of whack when a cup of coffee costs more than the daily newspaper

2244 restaurants which serve rabbit-sized portions, yet have the temerity to charge as if what they'd served was gold plated

2245 singing groups which comprise ten or more singers, but which perform mostly solos

2246 I've not been inside one, but I've always wondered what an EB Games shop is all about

2247 immediately after World War II, a BBC interviewer asked a German Luftwaffe pilot what it was like in the air; the German replied, 'Vell, I looks aboves me, and there's a f**ker, and I looks belows me, and there's another f**ker.' 'Oh,' shrieked the BBC man. 'I think what my esteemed guest means is there were Fokkers all around him.' 'Jawohl,' replied the German pilot, 'there was them too … but these f**kers was Spitfires.'

2248 no risk, no reward

2249 be alert but not alarmed

2250 stay calm and carry on

2251 bulltish

2252 the stupid ad where the cricketer stuffs half an avocado down his pants; anyone knows a cricket protector is white

2253 Tommy Cooper, arriving on stage to huge applause, asks, *'Do we have time for more?'*

2254 conspiring with my daughter to stop my granddaughter from saying 'like', which she does like three times in like every sentence

2255 Kass is amazed how many white people there are in Australia; she continually says, *'I'm so proud of your country, baby'*

2256 the way TV investigation shows replay the same part of the story over and over

2257 our supermarket no longer stocks chocolate-coated peanuts, but other outlets do

2258 the way breathalyser numbers tumble on TV police investigation shows, but cut to an ad before the numbers come to rest — and we viewers are left hanging — so damn annoying

2259 no one, and I mean *no one* will force me to wear my shirt tucked *out*

2260 am I, or am I not onto a good thing getting unlimited calls *and* data for $70 a month?

2261 the woman at the next pokie was betting $1.50 per spin and had a $149 balance (note: I bet 2c with a session limit of $10); she later left, penniless, looking utterly miserable

2262 in a previous marriage, I agreed to take dancing lessons, but the cute young (male) dance instructor with gorgeous dark brown eyes clearly had eyes only for me

2263 I don't understood how your family can overrule your *written* wish to donate organs

2264 the person who tried to wreck my career, but whom management later, finally, realised was an indescribable, incompetent waste of space (you can tell I'm still pissed)

2265 all of those times when I said yes but meant to say no — and have lived to regret it

2266 imagine what all of those hundreds of cricketers, footballers and basketballers would be doing if their sport had not been invented

2267 the Bible-reading footballer who accepted an illegal hand pass — but didn't fess-up!

2268 the bar I'm in has no fewer than twenty-two betting screens — I don't know which one to watch

2269 the young waiter who wished me happy holidays — when retirement is one long holiday

2270 3,000 Army Reservists are called out for 'Operation

Bushfire Assist 2019-20' — the first reservist call-out in Australia's history (with full work wages legislated)

2271 sadly, I wasn't included in this New Year's 'People To Watch' list in the newspaper, nor was I among those who received a gong in the Australia Day Honours List; next time

2272 feeling neglected, overlooked and thoroughly despondent

2273 quid pro quos

2274 tit for tats

2275 you scratch my back and I'll scratch yours; deal?

2276 *Sixty-eight million* people worldwide eat at McDonald's each day

2277 worldwide, McDonald's sells *seventy-five burgers every second*

2278 the Queen owns a McDonalds (the one closest to Buckingham Palace)

2279 the world's oldest person is 117; living another 46 years is the *last thing* I want to do

2280 the retailer's 'back-to-school' ad urges parents to come in and buy all the things their kids will *lose* in their first week back at school

2281 14,000 Vietnamese die on the roads annually; half the deaths are on motorbikes

2282 some hospital wards in Vietnam are named in honour of major motorcycle brands

2283 it's happened again; the waitress told me to take a seat, and she'd '… *be right over*'; she then went to the blackboard and rewrote the entire menu before finally taking my order

2284 we check our phone, on average, eighty times a day

2285 I know nothing about betting, nor do I care to, but it seems to be a total cop-out for the betting agency to offer the exact same odds for both teams — *they* certainly don't gamble

2286 I used Seasol on the tomatoes — and we now have seven fruit

2287 let's be honest about applauding those individuals who gave a decent sum to the bushfire appeal, but for whom it merely represented lunch money!

2288 truth vs spin — Trump's 25,000 lies

2289 deep or trivial

2290 webcamsydney.com gives a great live view of the Opera House and Harbour Bridge

2291 God is watching

2292 I don't understand why, if a tennis player throws or smashes his tennis racket, he isn't banned from all competitions for twenty-six years

2293 a cricketer who sledges another player using four-letter words should be rubbed out also for sixteen years — thirty-six years if the slur is homophobic

2294 the word is *'deterrent'* — it's been lacking in Australia's legal vocabulary for decades

2295 four out of five people in Coober Pedy live underground

2296 I'll choose to take on the chaser with the worst win rate

2297 I'm so much better at answering questions on *The Chase* when I recline my chair

2298 my daughter needs me to be her driver today, so I won't be attending parliament

2299 Tasmania's Bruny Island has 800 residents but 150,000 visitors, annually

2300 300,000 people visit Tasmania's Freycinet National Park and Wineglass Bay each year

2301 Tasmania has one naval vessel — a tiny little tugboat

2302 Tasmania gets $2.5 billion in GST revenue each year *plus* a recently announced extra huge top-up each year

2303 I never can get all ten differences in the two, side-by-side cartoons in the newspaper

2304 it's time I put on some clothes

2305 basketballer Ben Simmons is said to be getting $242m during his current contract

2306 I've decided to go viral

2307 I've decided to re-gift myself

2308 no way will I wear a device on my wrist which tells my family where I am

2309 a New Year's goal is for us to take Skybus to the Airport, choose two random seats on a random airline, and just go, go, go; no itinerary, no plans, no timeline, no buts

2310 how can the villages of Fr Brown and Midsomer have so many murders; impossible

2311 lavender scented kitchen tidy bags

2312 vanilla orchid scented air freshener

2313 expecting top-shelf aftershave in this year's Santa Stocking

2314 oysters — if only

2315 drinking green tea makes you live longer

2316 eating dark chocolate makes you live longer

2317 eating garlic makes you live longer but reduces your number of friends

2318 bring back Mrs McGillicuddy

2319 bring back Kylie Mole

2320 bring back Norman Gunston

2321 bring back Skippy

2322 bejesus means to express surprise, it has nothing to do with Christ

2323 surreal means bizarre, not unreal

2324 I suspect it's due to ageing, but on the No.70 tram, as it races past the tennis centre, I fear it will derail due to excessive speed, crash into one of the many concrete power poles close to the track, and the driver and all of us passengers will be killed dead

2325 why do I feel so indebted, beholden and subservient to publishers when I've done all of the damn work — and they make most of the money from my brilliance?

2326 my daughter posts on Facebook: *'I will never chase a man, but if he has tattoos and muscles a bitch might power-walk'* (how did all of my brilliant parenting come to this?)

2327 I think it's untrue, but the story goes that a visitor to the White House Christmas party asked the president what the 'J' in his name stood for. Trump replied, *'Genius'*

2328 businessman to politician: *'I know how to get you some money. I'll say something truly evil about you, you sue me for defamation, and I'll settle out of court for $2 million'*

2329 as I write this, the Aussie print book market has hit a low, its value falling by three per cent to $1.14 billion; good news however, is that *humour* book sales rose last year by 19%, so there's hope, yet

2330 I adore book publishers

2331 fingers crossed

2332 knock on wood

2333 God willing

2334 here's hoping

2335 Kass just spent $60 to have her nails done; I chew mine for zip

2336 Kass's popcorn and coke cost more than my movie ticket

2337 federal politician: 'It's a state issue'

2338 state politician: 'It's a federal issue'

2339 politician: 'I need to spend more time with my family'

2340 one-time Queensland premier: Sir Joh Bjelke Petersen: 'Don't you worry about that'

2341 more from Sir Joh: 'Goodness gracious, I know what you're trying to do. Just you wait and see.'

2342 ex-PM Tony Abbott, 'Look, I'm going to shirt-front Mr Putin ... you bet I am'

2343 'I would walk to Bourke backwards if the gay population of North Queensland is any more than 0.001%' — MP Bob Katter (his half-brother later came out as gay)

2344 spin

2345 smugness

2346 when it's much, much worse than you thought it would be

2347 movie scenes which make me weep: (1) King Richard identifying himself to Robin Hood in Sherwood Forest; (2) Dave telling the First Lady that his marriage didn't take; (3) the captain asking Maria in the gazebo from whom he should seek permission to marry her

2348 movies which make me weep again and again

2349 the Cloud

2350 wondering what Egg Boy has been up to lately?

2351 slofies

2352 hoi polloi

2353 knackered

2354 the time I entered the automatic car wash at the wrong end and the other driver was as startled as me

2355 *'As long as I have the microphone ...'*

2356 when you have true inspiration, words write themselves

2357 the Commonwealth Bank buying Shane Warne's baggy cap for $1,007,500 — oh my! what a wonderful corporate-charitable citizen the Bank is after all that messy business

2358 the nursing home ad which makes its facilities and services look like life at the Ritz, but is the daily meal allowance more than six dollars per resident?

2359 I told Kass that I love her, and she rolled her eyes, again

2360 the Officeworks ad where a dad gathers stationery for his daughter's school project, only for her to tell him she'll be doing a Power Point presentation — it makes the father look like a total dumb-arse, yet again (and where's the freaking mother?)

2361 Camp Sussex is yet to play its Trump card

2362 cometh the hour, cometh the woman

2363 I've decided it's a good idea to have the grandchildren attend my birthday dinner; that way, it means the meal will end earlier and I will get home to bed, sooner

2364 I asked her why, and she goes …

2365 people who travel *over* to another country ('over' is [totally] redundant)

2366 people who come *over* to Australia (ditto)

2367 knowing that the trees at our farm which I nurtured for so long and into which I poured my heart and soul, and hour upon hour of attention, will outlive me

2368 knowing that my two surviving children, who I so carefully nurtured for so long and into whom I poured my heart and soul (and all of my money), will outlive me

2369 a *fortnight* after my younger son died, a church minister asked me how I was coping. Not good, I told him, mournfully, tears welling. He replied, '*But it's been two weeks.*'

2370 when your elder child turns forty, you know your days are numbered

2371 the husband in the Temple & Webster TV ad is made to look like a total idiot

2372 when I'm on a hiding-to-nothing

2373 the talent in the Optus TV ad looks like a cross between John Howard and an M&M

2374 it's official: a 40-minute afternoon nap does wonders for one's cognitive performance

2375 henceforth, there will be more afternoon naps, like the good old days in kindergarten

2376 still waiting to be the near-naked stud on the front cover of a glossy magazine

2377 I didn't get Danube cruise tickets from Santa, but I did get a book of Sudoku puzzles

2378 and I got Kitty Flanagan's *488 Rules For Life* and Elton's *Me*; I can now die happy

2379 in early 2020 there were more than *298 separate bushfires* raging across Australia

2380 today's award goes to the bogan SUV driver who blocked a 'Keep Clear' grid, spread his vehicle across two lanes to stop people getting past, and then ran a red arrow

2381 back to the strife I had with the car — which cost $970 to fix — she now goes *beaudaful*

2382 good books which end

2383 dreadful books which never should have seen the light of day — and never end

2384 as I was saying

2385 any mistakes in this masterpiece were made in production, or meant to piss you off

2386 to my way of thinking, Airbnb is good for feral renters but a nightmare for owners

2387 when I have right of way, and the other driver doesn't pull over, I find it works best if I drive *straight at him*

2388 Uber is so unfair on taxi owners, who lost most of the value of their 'plates'

2389 could the world survive another four years of Trump in 2024?

2390 when a new suit comes with the pockets sewn up but with no cash inside the pockets

2391 recurring nightmares

2392 74% of students at the University of Wollongong admit to using drugs

2393 that the milk bar man didn't give the little girl a bit more change with the chocolate

2394 there wasn't a sequel to *The Thorn Birds*

2395 there won't be another Colleen McCullough

2396 oh, how I miss my Honda S600 soft top sports car — powered by a rubber band

2397 the American NRA and its far-right, moronic, gun-toting followers

2398 the placebo was fake news

2399 sport played on sacred days

2400 sacred days sold out to sport

2401 cage fighting

2402 indoctrination — all conceivable forms, especially educational, political, religious

2403 violence — all conceivable forms, especially against women and children

2404 one day, my screenplay of *Jackaroo* will be made into a movie

2405 one day, my second memoir will be published

2406 I'm nearing the end of my tether

2407 the price of books with pictures

2408 the price of books with running writing

2409 I don't care what you think

2410 I don't care what you say

2411 I don't care what you wear

2412 and I'd be most grateful if you'd pay me the same courtesy

2413 I must stop saying I don't care

2414 I've realised my passport has so many unstamped pages which will never be filled

2415 Pay Day loan providers! Would they let their mother take out such a loan?

2416 a copy of this book is going straight to the pool room, Darryl

2417 some people earn a million dollars; I write

2418 once, in a job application, I was asked if I ever took a (weekend) afternoon nap: I lied

2419 the visitor fee to London Tower is waived if you allow your pet dog to be the lions' lunch

2420 phew!

SCHOOL SCANDAL (2)

2421 Headmaster phones a groomed student to ask if he'll be wearing his school uniform to court — where his teacher is facing multiple charges. Then in court, a masterful barrister grills the 15-year-old victim for two days straight. Later at the same school, the deputy principal separately tells the school counsellor not to investigate a sexual abuse complaint because, if she does, she will ... *'damage the school's reputation'*

THINGS I WISH I'D KNOWN

I'm pissed off I didn't know these things (credits to Mental Floss & allthatsinteresting.com):

*

2422 four-year-olds on average ask 400 questions a day (little wonder parents get exhausted)

*

2423 fairy floss was invented by a dentist (talk about a clever way to drum up business!)

*

2424 the Queen has had more than thirty corgis

*

2425 54 million people who are alive right now will be dead in 12 months (comforting!)

2426 Sweden sends its blood donors a thank-you text message when their blood is used

2427 there are more cars than people in Los Angeles

2428 the inventor of the Pringles cardboard cylinder had his ashes buried inside one

2429 a Blue Whale's heart is the size of a car, its arteries wide enough to swim through

2430 a fan of Charles Bronson bequeathed all of her assets to him — valued at $300,000

2431 two-thirds of Africa is in the northern hemisphere

2432 Disney nearly named the dwarfs Chesty, Tubby, Burpy, Deafy, Hickey, Wheezy, Awful

2433 Facebook first considered calling the 'Like' button 'Awesome'

2434 on one day in April, 1930, the BBC decided there was no news, so it played music

2435 a mouse can squeeze through a hole the size of a ballpoint pen

2436 more people are obese than hungry

2437 Americans are more likely to become president than they are to win lotto

2438 bananas are berries

2439 when your mother was born, she was already carrying the egg that would become you

2440 goats have rectangular pupils (the ones in their eyes, not the ones in their classroom)

2441 mosquitoes have forty-seven teeth

2442 in 1999, a company called Excite passed on buying Google for less than $1 million

2443 multiple 'Marlboro Men' have died from lung cancer

2444 Ben and Jerry learned to make ice-cream from a five-dollar correspondence course

2445 the longest gap between the birth of twins is eighty-seven days

*

2446 in its first year of life a baby costs her parents 750 hours of sleep

*

2447 if 'The Simpsons' characters aged normally, Bart would be older than his mother in the first series

*

2448 more people in New York City bite *each other* than sharks worldwide bite people

*

2449 total ants outweigh total humans

*

2450 over *one million* Americans have made their dog the primary beneficiary in their will

*

2451 we regrow our entire skin every month

*

2452 avocados don't ripen on trees, making the trees an excellent storage facility

*

2453 Janis Joplin left $2,500 in her will for her friends to have a party

*

2454 the Queen is a qualified motor mechanic

*

2455 of all the people in history who've reached sixty-five years of age, half are living now

*

2456 aeroplane food lacks taste and smell because these senses drop by half during a flight

TAXPAYER ANGST

2457 The Grand Prix costs taxpayers $60 million. The 1996 Commonwealth Games cost us $1.1 billion. The Australian Institute of Sport's annual budget is $384 million. *WTF!*

I FAILED

This is not an easy story to tell. It concerns my biggest ever failure. Admitting defeat even after twenty years still pisses me off, because (a) I let people down, (b) failure made me look stupid, and (c) I think my brilliant idea still is do-able — by someone else!

2458 I had long held a cheeky thought, that setting a Guinness World Record for the world's biggest choir would be a fun thing to do. Here in Melbourne. At the mighty MCG. I called the idea the 'Great Australian Sing' (GAS). I got in touch with the people at Guinness, who kindly sent their guidelines. The record attempt would involve filling the MCG stands and playing surface with **110,000** choristers. (English soccer crowds singing their club anthem are ineligible, apparently.) I contacted a friend who ran an event management business. He and his business partner promptly agreed to manage the event. 'I' had now become 'we'. Next, we set up a non-profit foundation. A senior Victorian judge agreed to be the chairman of the board, and another twelve prominent Melbournians signed on to lend their name and time to be on the board, and have their name on the letterhead. A television network liked the idea of televising the event, which was essential. The Melbourne Cricket Club liked it, and pencilled in a date for us to use the MCG. We then secured a well-known choral identity to be the musical director and conductor. Aligning the sound of 110,000 voices was a worry until a leading sound specialist said, without concern, that each choir would need to be microphoned. From where would singers come? On the basis that an average school/church/community choir comprises fifty singers, we would need to enlist 2,200 choirs from across Australia and New Zealand. Rotary and other service clubs would be asked to accommodate the choristers. So, what went wrong? Due to difficult things happening in my personal life, I suffered a severe breakdown. My brilliant idea didn't eventuate. But I truly believe it is still possible to achieve this dream! Someone step up.

BUCKET LIST

I will be mightily pissed off if I fail to achieve the following before I snuff it ...

2459 visit a yoghurt factory, watch it being made, leave with a truckload of free samples

2460 speak at the Melbourne Writers Festival

2461 convince my son and daughter-in-law to send their children to a *government* school

2462 have dinner with Jim Chalmers and Penny Wong

2463 receive an application form from God

2464 revisit Governors' Camp in Kenya's Masai Mara, this time with Kass

2465 cruise Alaska's coastal waters

2466 cruise the Danube River (on a cruise line which promises no kids, no casinos)

2467 cruise anywhere else in the world which costs an absolute freaking fortune

2468 win lotto and buy that houseboat — oh, and a top-shelf motorhome

2469 snorkel the Great Barrier Reef — and post a letter home at its out-at-sea mailbox

2470 compete on *The Chase Australia* — and win!

2471 enjoy a sandwich lunch with Barack and Michelle Obama

2472 travel on the world's agreed top ten railway journeys, first class

2473 share afternoon tea with Sir Elton John and his family

2474 watch bank notes being made — and pocket the odd note which falls on the floor

2475 teach a writing class

2476 stay a fortnight in an English country pub — and drink copious pints of Pommy beer

2477 sit in on a federal government cabinet meeting — and be asked my opinion, *often*

2478 have this book published to rave reviews

2479 share a tuna and mayo sandwich lunch with Her Majesty (crusts off)

2480 see a Royal Variety Performance from the Royal Box with a few Royals seated behind

2481 tour a whisky distillery where the tour guide falls ill and leaves us to our own devices

MESSY BUSINESS

As a teenage jackaroo on a sheep station I was made to castrate lambs — using my teeth!

2482 It was the first week of winter, and we three jackaroos were sent to a distant paddock to install a set of portable sheep yards, for the annual lamb 'marking', whatever that meant. I was a city boy; I had no idea. The set-up included 50 metres of wire netting angled out into the paddock, to act as a kind of funnel to guide poor unsuspecting sheep into the yards. By the time we jackaroos arrived at the site the next morning at five o'clock, the manager, with the help of his trusty sheep dog and his Land Rover's headlights, had already mustered the sheep, and was pushing them up the funnel-trap, into the yards. We drafted (separated) the ewes from their lambs, then let the mothers back into the paddock. But they didn't go far; they hovered close by, bleating frantically for their babies. We then forced the first fifty or so lambs into a catching pen, about the size of a small car. I watched as my fellow jackaroos each picked up a lamb, held it by its four legs, and sat it on the outer rail. I followed their lead and caught a mid-size lamb. First to come by was a station hand with injection pack in hand. He inoculated each lamb under its foreleg. He was followed by another station hand who used a metal device, like a pair of pliers but with teeth, to cut a notch in the lamb's ear: left ear for boys, right ear for girls. Finally, the manager used his pocket knife to slice off the tail, although if the lamb was a boy, he first cut open the little guy's fluffy scrotum; he then flicked the knife backwards under his wrist. Next, using his thumb and fingers, he squeezed the sack so the oblong testicles poked out. He then bent over, clamped his teeth behind the two objects, stood up, and drew out the testicles along with a heap of sinews. His face was covered in copious blood. Horrified, and feeling for the poor little guy, I squeezed my knees together, tightly. On the third day of this bizarre and warped craziness, they made me do it.

Footnote: today's graziers use rubber rings, which cause the testicles to fall off in a fortnight.

SUPERMARKETS (2)

Have you heard of SWIPERS?

2483 'Seemingly Well-Intentioned Persons Engaged in Routine Shoplifting' — in other words, supermarket shoppers who commit fraud at self-serve checkout machines. *'It's cheating, not stealing,'* argued one young offender. Like it was all just a game.

2484 Apparently, 80% of university students swipe expensive vegetables as carrots. One supermarket found it had been selling more carrots than they had in stock!

2485 People are so stupid. One guy tried to scan two kilos of fish — as onions.

2486 Another shopper tried to get away with scanning a whole chicken — as bananas!

2487 Yet another rort included scanning a $20 cake from the bakery — as bread rolls.

2488 Or weighing pink lady apples ($5 per kilo) — as watermelon ($1 per kilo).

2489 Or coloured, Krispy Kreme donuts — as plain ones.

2490 One young person said he did it to see what he could *get away with*!

2491 A Queensland woman was jailed after defrauding a supermarket of $4,500. Thirty-one times, she'd stuck the barcodes from items she'd previously taken home onto items she took off the shelves on her next visit — onto items like meat, protein powder; even onto a coffee machine which was on special!

2492 In some supermarkets, management limits self-serve shopping to twelve items as a way to stem the cost of theft, which one supermarket put at $1.1 billion per year.

2493 Getting rid of human checkout staff must be worthwhile, however, given each self-serve machine costs around $150,000. And they keep installing more and more machines!

2494 the downside to these otherwise clever machines is constantly having to call for help.

2495 The worst crime I've committed is to genuinely forget to scan the 15c plastic bag.

PAY TV

Do you subscribe to Pay TV, or, like me, do you object to the whole thing on principle?

2496 I flatly refuse to *pay* to watch TV — I've been watching free-to-air TV since the day it began in Australia, in 1956, and I don't plan on changing my ways any time soon. Back in 1956, those of us who couldn't afford to buy a TV would gather and watch a TV in a shop window; we all stood there out on the street. It was kind of cathartic; community building.

2497 These days, it is so annoying to read about a great-sounding show coming soon, only to get to the bottom of the review, and read: 'Stan, Thursday, 7.30 pm.'

2498 Who the hell is Stan?

2499 Okay, so I may be a slow learner, but I'm gradually learning to skip the pages in the weekly TV guide headed: 'PAY TV' or 'Streaming', whatever streaming means.

2500 *Hey, Ms Editor, I don't want to read about shows I can't afford to watch.*

2501 I guess I'm stuck with reruns of M.A.S.H. and Murder She Wrote.

2502 Or maybe I need to find an alternative to watching TV. Like writing a book.

*

2503 Then there's sport. Almost all sport is morphing onto Pay TV. I thought there was an agreement between government and sporting bodies that major sports were to remain the province of free-to-air TV. It was called 'anti-siphoning'. They've gone silent on that. (Back in the day, 'anti-siphoning' meant preventing people from stealing your petrol.)

2504 Pay TV is a joke. Once again, the small guy, the pensioner — me — gets screwed.

SIGN LANGUAGE

2505 Did you know that when the Queen wants to be rescued from a boring conversation, she signals to a nearby aide by switching her handbag to her other arm?

DRIVING (2)

2506 Victoria Police crushes *six* impounded hoon cars *each day*. That's a staggering 2,190 cars crushed per year. I didn't know there were that many hoons (and hoon cars) in Victoria!

*

2507 Have you arrived home after a day's work and thought, 'Well, I got through today without being hit by an ice addict, crushed by a semitrailer, crashed into by a drunk driver, back-ended by a tailgater, or pinged for doing 4 km/hr over a 40km/hr speed limit?'

*

2508 I get mad when a driver indicates he's moving into my lane — after he's done it.

*

2509 Despite the warnings and threats of $1,000 fines,

millennials continue to overtake me, head down, texting.

*

2510 A full ashtray once was sufficient grounds to trade in one's car. Today, it's a flat tyre, a spider crawling across the dashboard, or a minor dent caused by a flying cricket ball.

*

2511 On the Monash Freeway, a bogan motorcyclist in flapping, flannel shorts and a short-sleeved shirt overtook me doing at least 150 km/hr. I watched him disappear into the distance, weaving in and out of lanes, willy-nilly; I wonder if he made it to Berwick, alive!

*

2512 While this was happening, all I saw in my rear vision mirror was the massive silver grille of a huge semitrailer, tailgating me — travelling no more than three metres behind me.

*

2513 At the time of writing, I still have my smarts, but how long will it be before my son decides I'm beyond driving — like I did to my mother — and he confiscates my car keys?

GRAMMAR

2514 Every so often the principal of my school sends an email to alumni. In a recent email, she wrote, 'In the meantime, Penny, Jeremy and myself will ...' Goodness gracious. The only thing worse than the bad grammar — it should be 'Penny, Jeremy and I ...' — is (a) it came from the principal, no less, and (b) there is no one at the school to proofread her material.

*

2515 I mentioned earlier the print journalist who regularly speaks on radio and who used 'um' a staggering *sixty-four times* in a *four-minute* report. I cannot believe no one took her aside and told her it is possible to avoid saying um by concentrating on each word you say. And to tell yourself, 'I will *not* use um in what I'm about to say.' It is so annoying.

*

2516 Kass calls from work, saying, *'I'm going home soon.'* Of course it should be *'coming'*, but I love the way she says things the way she does; I have no intention of correcting her.

*

2517 Likewise, the way the wonderful ex-footy player-turned-commentator, the late Jack Dyer, used to say on air, *'He come on the field at half time, he done, and he give 'em buggery.'* We wouldn't have changed dear old Jack for quids; he was one in a million.

WOKE & BESPOKE

2518 If you're over (let's say) sixty, like me, the words 'woke' and 'bespoke' must annoy the living crap out of you. What gives? Apparently, woke means awake, as in 'We need to stay woke.' So why not say so? Then there's bespoke, which I'm told means 'made especially for you'. Again, why not say so? It's stupid, yet I fear I'm too late. I need to curl up and die!

RULES

2519 Having parked my car by the river, next to a cute little jetty, I pushed the button on the car CD and began to listen to Celine Dion. I soaked up the beauty of the surrounding landscape. A short time later, a car pulled up near me. A mother and two young boys got out. Within moments, the boys were diving off the end of the jetty. Then another car arrived. This time, it was a father and three young boys. I guessed the boys were school friends, because they all were wearing the same yellow shirt. The two adults watched on as the five boys proceeded to do water-bombs off the jetty. It pissed me off, because next to the jetty a council notice declared diving off the jetty, prohibited. I know it wasn't the world's worst crime, but what kind of message, what kind of lesson was this breach of local government by-laws teaching those five young kids (assuming they could read or had even noticed the sign)? I'm not suggesting disobeying a by-law necessarily will lead to a life of rampant crime, alcohol abuse, drug use or wife bashing. But if we don't teach our children and grandchildren to obey the simplest of society's conventions (like reading a bloody sign) and rules (obeying the sign), what hope is there? Or am I just an old fart, far beyond my use-by date?

YES, MINISTER

2520 All three stars of *Yes Minister* are dead. Paul Eddington died in 1995, aged 68; Nigel Hawthorne in 2001, aged 72; Derek Fowlds in 2020, aged 82. Writers Jonathan Lynn is 77, but Antony Jay died in 2016, aged 86. Said Jay, *'In defeat, malice. In victory, revenge.'*

AGED POO!

Everyone has a favourite poo story, the aim being to horrify the listener or reader.

2521 On a recent country drive, we passed a farmer's roadside stall selling not just poo, but *aged* poo. I guess one is expected to read *aged* as *quality*. Do plants really need *aged* poo? Surely, poo is poo, although aged poo I guess must be top-shelf stuff. Next, they'll try to sell us aged water!

*

2522 My all-time, best poo story happened when I was two. We lived with my mother's parents, and I smeared a large amount of my fresh poo all over the white wall next to my cot. My mean and nasty grandmother hated me, and smearing poo on her wall was my joyous revenge. When I became older and I could understand things better, my mother said my grandmother didn't relate to me because I was a boy, and she didn't *understand* boys because she'd only had a girl — my mother. What a load of crap! What was there to not comprehend? Her husband had a penis; he must have used it once, at least. To this day, I feel pleased that my poo smearing angered my horrid grandmother so much. Another way I knew my grandmother hated me was because whenever she could, she'd arrange for my pram — with me in it — to be placed under the big lemon tree in her back garden, a lemon tree which, incidentally, grew gigantic lemons. From my pram, I could see my grandmother standing at the kitchen window, willing a big, hard and heavy lemon to fall on my head. And kill me. It's amazing that one didn't. Later, when I could walk and talk, we had Sunday lunches at my grandparents' house. Sunday lunch always was roast beef and Yorkshire pudding — standard English fare. I was not allowed seconds of Yorkshire pudding. My sister Penny, however, was allowed as many helpings as she could stuff into her mouth. And she was pudding size. Penny also was allowed to learn the piano, yet music was considered not a manly thing for me. I got around the ban in boarding school, but that's another story.

UNPARLIAMENTARY

I'm passing over this gripe to young Justin, from Canberra, and for him to tell it his way:

2523 Hi! My name is Justin. I'm like fourteen, and I'm in year 9 at St John's College, in Canberra. Yesterday, we went to Parliament House, to watch Question Time. Last week, they took us to the Australian War Memorial, where all of us were like blown away by the amount of people killed in wars — like all of those names on walls, some really young, too. Yesterday was different. We'd been warned by the teachers that Question Time can be robust (I had to ask me dad what robust meant). We made our way to what's called the House of Representatives chamber (room), where everything is like pastel green. I was just metres from Mr Morrison (he's the only politician I've ever heard of). Everyone was quiet while the man who sat in the big chair at the end — he's called the Speaker — read a prayer. He then called on the PM to say something. Everyone was silent while Mr Morrison read a speech about how we need to kill terrorists before they kill us. After he finished, a man across from him got a turn. He talked about the Australians who died in the London Bridge attack, and the man who got killed in Melbourne. When all of that was over, Mr Speaker announced Question Time, and straight away all of the politicians went like feral and began to yell at each other. It was like school assembly before the teachers arrive, but lots worse. After 10 minutes, I couldn't stand it any longer. When the person speaking finished, I stood up and yelled out: *'Why don't you all grow up? We're a bunch of school kids and we're nowhere near as bad as you.'* The place went like mega quiet, and then a man in a brown and green uniform came and told me to follow him. I got taken to the front door, where a teacher was waiting. He looked real mad. Back at school, the principal listened to what had happened, and then said he needed to give me a Friday detention, even though he didn't really want to. Then the TV cameras arrived and like everything went pear-shaped for the principal because of what he'd said about not wanting to give me the detention.

LOVE LANGUAGES

Few books made me think as much as Dr Gary Chapman's 'The Five Love Languages'. I'm pissed off that I didn't know about it a whole lot earlier.

2524 Dr Chapman's bestselling self-help book says when it comes to our relationship with our partner, we use five languages. (I'm not about to name the five languages here, because to do so would be unfair on Dr Chapman, and probably illegal. But I can talk in general terms about the issue.) Dr Chapman invites us to consider the five languages — the five different ways we relate to our partner — and to work on the 'language' which we think is most important to him/her. He then asks us to consider which language best applies to us, and encourage our partner to work on that language. Vacuuming isn't a language, but it gets mentioned a lot. Females so wish their male partner would do the vacuuming — even once — without being asked. Voluntarily. A close friend, Judy, has spent most of her adult life on the land with her husband. Judy loved Dr Chapman's book so much, she gathered together nine other farming 'widows'; they met one morning a week, over several weeks, having coffee in their local pub, and they worked through the book, page by page. Judy says the women all resonated completely with Dr Chapman's message. Even regarding the issue of vacuuming! The problem was, Sally later told me, the menfolk wouldn't get off their tractors long enough to follow the story. Nor would the men read the book in bed at night. For these women, unfortunately, the exercise failed, even though they'd each learned valuable lessons for the future. Next time, they'd be well prepared, thanks to *The Five Love Languages*.

DEMENTIA (1)

2525 an elderly woman being helped to the toilet by a male nurse: *'It's been such a long time since I've had a young man take down my pants'*

WALKING THE CAMINO

You know how, when you've done something special, you want to share the story? But no one shows any interest in your incredible experience. It pisses you right off! Yes?

2526 One of many special things I've done, which I wanted to share with you, was trekking the Camino de Compostela de Santiago pilgrim trail, in Spain. I did it in 2013, and I highly recommend it (even though each year it seems to be increasingly trashed by bogans). I'm also pissed that now, seven years after my walk, I feel too old and slow to do it again! You don't need to be religious to walk the Camino: for exercise is good enough reason. I'm still kicking myself that I didn't trek the entire 800 km. I managed only 543 km. Walking on flat ground or downhill I found easy; it was walking uphill I found difficult. Twice, I caught a bus to avoid steep hills. Ever since, I've felt terribly guilty. Early one morning, in the dark, I took a wrong turn on the otherwise well-marked Camino track (yellow arrows everywhere). I ended up walking on a disused highway, a two-metre-high cyclone fence on either side to prevent my escape. I kept walking. Three times, I looked behind me and saw, one hundred metres back, a man dressed all in black, following me. He wore a huge broad-brimmed black hat, conjuring an image of St James, the apostle, in whose memory the Camino is dedicated. (St James's remains, according to successive popes, are preserved in a crypt in the Santiago Cathedral). Seeing the man scared me, and so another three times I spun round to look, but he'd gone. I continued walking until I came to a roundabout, where I sat on a rock, and waited. But the man never came. Was he a real person? Was he St James? Had he been there all along to protect me? There are many miracles recorded about the Camino de Santiago de Compostela pilgrimage — like the one about the headless chook dancing on a mayor's lunch table — you can choose to believe them, or not. Each day I met and walked with new people from all corners of the world. Each night I slept in a different Alberg (dormitory). My account of my trek — **'27 Days A Pilgrim'** — is available as an e-Book at www.amazon.com.

REUNIONS & FUNERALS

Do you attend school reunions? Can you be bothered? Does the very thought piss you off?

2527 Last year, I attended a lunch for our class of 1966. We all are seventy-one — a worry! There were 135 boys in our all-boy year group. Twenty-one have died. Prior to attending the reunion, I had numerous concerns. Had I done *as well* in life as my contemporaries? How would I *look* compared to my peers? Did I have enough in common with them to get through an entire lunch, stuck in a room together? I shared my concerns with a classmate, who tried to reassure me. '*Michael,*' said Doug, '*we're no longer competitive; our sole goal now is to stay alive!*' The lunch was pleasant enough, and it was interesting to hear others' stories and see who among us had survived the journey best, physically. Financially, we'd never know! Certainly, I'd not made a lot of money, but then I hadn't started out with as much as others, either. I'm sure I wasn't the most haggard-looking in our class. Doug had warned me that two topics of conversation were banned: *health* and *marriage*. That was fine by me. Health is boring, and I didn't want to have to confess to three marriages, the present one to a gorgeous 33-year-old Filipino *GUY!* How schooling has changed. Imagine, in 1966, telling a teacher, *'Sir, I don't want to go to the School Dance, because I'm gay — and you won't let me take a boy!'* Of the twenty-one class mates who've died, the most recent was last month. Richard, so I learned from the informative, moving eulogies and well-attended funeral, was a highly-regarded barrister (I remember him being a super-bright boy at school). Outside work, he'd established a residential 'college' for university students from the bush, kids who couldn't afford the traditional college accommodation. His 'college' still operates today, and its graduates, as one, remain in awe and wonderment of their benefactor. There must have been 300 mourners present at Richard's funeral, including six members of our class. Some of us reflected that we'd known Richard longer than anyone else present, given we'd all been at kindergarten — and through all of school — together. Vale, Richard. Nice guy; much missed.

CONCUSSION

Football radio commentator: 'Are you allowed to deliberately bash people in the head?'

2528 The commentator had witnessed an AFL player receive a deliberate and crushing blow to the head. The problem with head injuries in body contact sports, notably all forms of rugby and Australian Rules Football, is that to be a champion player — and be admired by tens of thousands of the games' most ardent supporters — you need to be prepared and willing to run head-first into a pack of tough and solidly built human beings, to gain possession of the ball. Hawthorn legend Leigh Matthews, idolised by thousands, was famous for his courage. Fortunately, he survived — and still has his marbles. Some experts assert that all forms of AFL and rugby will be gone — finished — in ten years. That's hard to believe, given these sports' current followings — and the money involved. In the AFL, the incidence of concussion is six episodes per 1,000 playing hours. AFL is listed alongside boxing and rugby as extremely high-risk sports. In fairness to the AFL, it is now starting to address the problem. Clubs are now fined if a player, deemed to have been concussed, is sent back on the field. In a recent case, a club was fined $20,000 for a breach of this new rule. To a lay person, someone who likes to watch skilful players but not thugs, it seems incomprehensible that the most delicate part of the human body — the brain — can be placed in so much potential harm. I guess the inducement of earning $1,000,000 a year for seven years is worth the risk. You know, like all things potentially bad for people's health, I reckon the authorities know only too well all of the inherent dangers in the sport they administer. But, as usual, the pocket is mightier than a player's welfare. Would these administrators want their son or daughter to be subjected to such potential danger, so much harm? The answer, of course, is yes — because time and time again we see sons of ex-footballers being selected for their first AFL game. Just don't mention the word concussion.

GLEN CAMPBELL

Do certain deaths sadden you more than others? They do, me.

2529 I was particularly saddened by the passing of renowned country singer Glen Campbell. His singing voice – to this baby-boomer, at any rate – was pure magic. I shall never forget his concert at Melbourne's Festival Hall, in 1972. It was a freezing midwinter's night when four of us piled into a fellow agricultural college student's seriously unreliable bomb of a car, and we made the three-hour journey from Terang (in Victoria's western district), to Melbourne. All four of us were serious Glen Campbell fans. Glen was brilliant. His pitch perfect, twanging voice resounded throughout what was then considered to be Melbourne's premier entertainment centre. Showing my age, eh? He sang (his) real songs, songs with real lyrics: 'By the time I get to Phoenix', 'Gentle on my mind', 'Rhinestone cowboy', 'Wichita lineman', 'Galveston', 'Try a little kindness'. All so, so melodic; so, so lyrical; so, so sweet.

And then he sang his own arrangement of 'The Lord's Prayer'. Imagine singing *The Lord's Prayer* at a pop concert today! After his 'Good Time Hour' TV show in the US ran out of puff, in 1972, Glen hit the bottle. He spent many years in the depths of alcoholism. But he recovered, enough to resume touring. He then allowed his story to be told, warts and all – 'uncut' – as they say. It was a gripping and extremely raw documentary. Also on YouTube is 'Let It Be Me', sung live with his daughter, Debby, before he succumbed to dementia. There's a sad clip on YouTube of Glen in concert starting to repeat 'By The Time I Get To Phoenix' immediately after he'd just sung it! There was no way to hide it. *'Dad,'* said Debby live on stage, *'we just did it.'* At the time of his death, Glen was over his alcoholism, but the dementia got him, finally. Rest in peace, Glen Travis Campbell (1936-2017). You were great. It pisses me off big time that you've gone. Try a little kindness, everyone.

GAMBLING

2530 When I was a boy, Melbourne had a sensational weekly newspaper, Truth. No one admitted to reading the salacious rag, despite its 400,000-strong circulation. The same thing happens today with gambling. No one admits to betting, yet four out of five Aussies do it. Such lies, we tell. I've always felt the worst thing a gambler can do is to get an early win, because it makes it all look too easy. I was eighteen, spending a year working in England, when a work colleague invited me to his golf club. In the corner of the bar was a lonely slot machine, the first I'd ever seen (it was 1968). It had a long handle which you pulled down. My friend encouraged me to have a shot. I inserted a pound's worth of coins, and quickly lost all but five pence. Then, on my final spin, out poured twelve quid. Too easy!

*

2531 I truly believe poker machines have a hidden camera, and, using facial recognition, they capture a photo of our face when we sit down to play, They then match our image with our normal betting routine: how long we play, our average loss per session, and how often a small win is needed to keep us seated at a machine. All of this to maximise our losses, and a final losing amount far greater than our self-imposed session limit. Or am I totally paranoid?

2532 I once organised a work lunch for about forty business people. During the meal, I asked the chap next to me what he did for a living. *'I'm a professional gambler,'* he answered. I was intrigued. *'Really?'* I said. I hope I wasn't being rude. We chatted on, and then I said, *'I have a question: do you ever buy a lotto ticket?'* *'Yes I do,'* he replied. *'But why?'* I begged to know, *'when you, more than anyone, know the appalling odds against winning?'* And he replied, *'Because I'm buying two weeks of HOPE.'* Hard to argue with that!

CROSSING THE EQUATOR

I continue to be pissed off that I'm unable to exact revenge over a certain bunch of people.

2533 It happened when I was five. We were aboard the Dominion Monarch passenger liner bound for England for my father's work. He was a wool buyer — and an alcoholic. It was a beautiful, sunny day when the ship's passengers gathered at the swimming pool to watch the time-honoured event known as 'Crossing the Line' (crossing the Equator). Everyone was dressed in their finest; even the captain looked spiffing in his bleached whites. Yet, despite the pretty surrounds, bad things were happening. Innocent passengers were being plucked from the crowd by gorilla-like warriors, men with multicoloured war paint smeared across their gross bodies; men who I later learned were fare paying passengers, like us. I was as scared as any five-year-old could be, and I clung tightly to my mother's skirt for protection.

Alas, to no avail. About 20 minutes into this serious madness, a warrior headed towards *me*. He placed a fat, greasy hand on my precious head, and he used his other hand to prise my arms from my mother's legs. I thought of yelling for my father, but he was in a bar, getting drunk. My molester lifted me onto his shoulders, and headed towards King Neptune. I screamed. 'It's alright, Michael,' I heard my mother call out. '*He won't hurt you.*' Won't hurt me? The mongrel was about to have me for lunch. I was placed on a large table, where the king's men used brooms to lather me with soap suds. I was to be washed before being eaten. I lashed out with my right foot, hitting a fatso in his privates. He reeled back, and the crowd hushed. I don't think I was meant to do that. The other three warriors picked me up by my hands and ankles, and tossed me into the pool, whereupon I sank to the bottom. When I surfaced, another bunch of aquatic gorillas chased me to the water's edge, from where I was able to effect my escape. I'd got off lightly. Once, aboard an Australian Navy ship, a sailor drowned from this senseless ritual.

HEALTH SCARE

2534 It happened to me on a recent Saturday morning. I was sitting on the lounge, when all of a sudden, I realised I had no idea *who* I was, *where* I was, or *what I was doing*. It was all very scary. Kass emerged from the bedroom, and said, *'You look terrible.'* 'Thanks,' I replied. *'I don't know what day it is. Who are you?'* I tried to reason things. I knew we were due to meet a friend for lunch, in Geelong. But I was frozen on the couch, stuck in a time warp, my eyes fixed on the carpet. I couldn't move. *'Have you eaten breakfast?'* Kass asked. I said I'd had a bowl of cereal. Forty minutes later, we were driving along Flinders Street, towards the West Gate Bridge, when I realised I needed to pull over. *'I can't do this,'* I said. *'I don't know which lane I'm in.'* We sat there, me feeling completely disoriented and confused. Then, suddenly, my brain began to click in, such that when safe to do so, I was able to perform a U-turn. We drove to my doctor, taking it one street at a time. Fortunately, my GP was on duty, and seeing him gave me great comfort. He promptly instructed me to go to the Epworth (hospital), in Richmond. *'How will you get there?'* he asked. *'I can drive,'* I replied. *'It's over there,'* I said, pointing south with my right hand over my left shoulder. At the Epworth, the doctor who examined me said I was suffering global temporary amnesia. He told me it would pass in a few hours. Then he added, *'Best not to drive to Geelong today.'* Lunch duly got cancelled, and by three o'clock, I knew who I was again.

DEMENTIA (2)

2535 A woman suffering from dementia kept referring to her late husband in the present tense. *'But dad's been dead for thirty years,'* said her son. *'Well, then,'* replied the woman, *'Who was the person I climbed over this morning to get out of bed?'*

BULLYING

Sometimes, I get really pissed off at myself for not taking a stand.

2536 Once, I found myself on a bus along with a bunch of school kids. What looked like a year 9 boy shifted seats to sit next to another boy from the same school (same blazers). Straight away, the recipient boy got up and moved to a different part of the bus. I looked at the boy who'd been rejected, and I saw the hurt he was suffering. I felt the sharp knife that the unkind boy had driven through the friendly boy's heart. The hurt boy didn't know where to look, which made for more awkwardness. Lots of adult passengers were watching, although we all pretended not to stare. I then looked at the other boy, the boy who'd done the rejecting. He was now talking to friends further down the bus. Anger consumed me. I so wanted to punish the mean boy for his bullying, because that's what it was: nothing short of bullying. I wanted to tell the bully that he should learn about, and to be wary of something called karma — what goes round, comes round. About which, clearly, he had much to learn. The offending boy got off the bus at the next stop. And there was his mother, waiting for him in the family Volvo. Yes, I thought to myself, that'd be right: a Volvo driver.

*

2537 Q. What's the difference between an echidna and a Volvo? A. The echidna has the pricks on the outside.

*

2538 I'm still angry with myself that I hadn't spoken up and told the bully he was a piss-weak little turd. And, while it's no longer the done thing, given the abused kid a cuddle.

*

2539 I'm keen to know what happened to the three professors who called out their university for enrolling unqualified students (to maximise its income) — such as the international Masters-in-IT student who didn't know what a UBS stick is.

GOOD OLD TV

I so wish a free-to-air TV channel would devote an entire weekend to showing re-runs of:

2540 Bonanza

2541 Dennis the Menace

2542 Father Knows Best

2543 Gunsmoke

2544 Have Gun Will Travel

2545 Hopalong Cassidy

2546 I Love Lucy

2547 Jet Jackson

2548 Leave it to Beaver

2549 Maverick

2550 Rawhide

2551 Rin Tin Tin

2552 Superman

2553 The Cisco Kid

2554 The Ed Sullivan Show

2555 The Jackie Gleeson Show

2556 The Lone Ranger

2557 The Mickey Mouse Club

2558 The Perry Como Show

2559 The Red Skelton Show

2560 The Rifleman

2561 The Texas Rangers

2562 Wyatt Earp

JOB APPLICATIONS

I've been helping a nephew in the Philippines to improve his résumé and cover letter:

2563 Gaps in work history. During my consulting career, I helped numerous employers to hire staff. On one occasion, we, the interview panel, noted a year's gap in a candidate's work history. He explained it as a typo! We hired him, and not long after, he stole a swag of company money. The year's gap in the résumé turned out to be a 12-month stint in prison.

2564 Photo. Candidates often go to great lengths to make their photo look extra special. But how you look doesn't make you perform a job any better; it's your skill levels which count.

2565 Poor layout. Use of fancy fonts, using smaller typefaces to pack more in, and colour, all are to be avoided. And while cheeky email addresses might be smart at university, employers don't like them. Keep your email address boring, and conservative.

2566 Length. Long-winded résumés are a turn-off for busy HR personnel. Your document should be no longer than two pages, and to the point. Where you need to address given key strengths, list them one by one and use dot points to include specific achievements.

2567 Poor spelling and grammar. Do not rely on spellcheck. Nothing turns off employers more than grammatical and spelling errors, especially when the candidate claims attention-to-detail as a key strength.

2568 Cover letter. While you might use the same template for different applications, addressing your cover letter to a previous recipient won't get you very far.

DON'T MESS WITH STAFF

2569 The man one ahead of me at the airport check-in counter was so rude to the agent, such that when it was my turn, I apologised on the man's behalf. 'It's okay,' replied the agent, with a cheeky smile, '*He's going to Adelaide; his bags are going to Brisbane.*'

FISHY TALE

I've told you I once had a houseboat on Lake Eildon; no longer having it pisses me off.

2570 Friends Geoff and Judy Chesterman also had a houseboat at Eildon. On Friday nights, they would close their retail shop in Melbourne early so they could get to the Lake before dark. They'd then motor to a favourite cove, where they would tie up to the bank, and enjoy a quiet weekend. Things continued like that until one night last summer. A truly frightening event occurred. Geoff and Judy, along with their adored Maltese, Pebbles, arrived at their favourite cove only to find two houseboats already there. They continued on to their second favourite inlet. After securing the ropes, Geoff poured a whisky for himself and a brandy for Judy, and the couple moved to the upper deck to relax and enjoy the fresh country air. Pebbles ran upstairs, too. Later, they heard a loud thud. Geoff went to the side and peered over. 'It's okay,' he told Judy, *'just a carp* *swimming nearby; it must have hit a pontoon.*' Pebbles barked. More thuds, which came from downstairs. Geoff went to investigate. Pebbles followed. When Geoff got to the door leading to the back deck, he couldn't believe what he saw. Three huge carp had slithered in through Pebbles's doggy door and were tossing about on the hallway carpet. Another carp pushed itself through the doggy door. Then another. Geoff called to Judy to bring the broom. With broom in hand, he opened the door – a big mistake. A dozen more slippery carp came crashing in onto the carpet. Pebbles squeezed his way out onto the back deck while Geoff continued to spoon the carp out, until finally he was able to slam the door – and Pebbles's doggy door – shut. Judy called out to Pebbles. No answer! Geoff ran to the staircase, grabbing a torch from the kitchen bench as he went by. From the top deck, Geoff made broad sweeps with the torch. And there on the water's surface, metres away from the houseboat, the light shone on a thin strip of red leather, with small silver studs. The carp had taken Pebbles.

TRULY?

I need to explain the gripe I made earlier about why Americans give generously to charity.

2571 It has to do with their taxation system. Americans receive huge tax breaks for their donations, which encourages them to be so generous with the money they give away. Here's what I mean: John and Betty have no children, but what they do have is a holiday home at the seaside. The decide to gift the holiday home to John's school, but on the strict proviso that no one from the school is to set foot on the property, or make any changes to it, until after both John and Betty die. However, because the property is now owned by a not-for-profit organisation (John's school), they no longer have to pay council rates. John and Betty then decide to add a second storey to the house, to give themselves a better view of the ocean. All of the building materials, and the labour costs, are tax-deductible, because the home is now owned by a not-for-profit. With nothing to lose but everything to gain, leaving their holiday home to the school makes good practical — and financial — sense. What a rort!

*

2572 it's so annoying how, in the Philippines, movie goers talk loudly during the movie

*

2573 how much would the big hospital appeal raise if punters knew the top ten salaries?

*

2574 in 2019, four AFL coaches stood down, but not one club president did

*

2575 due to climate change, there will be an earthquake and a major skyscraper will fall

*

2576 'That shirt you're wearing looks like something the cat brought in; look at the cat'

*

2577 sign at McDonald's: 'Now hiring smiling feces'

*

2578 correct use of the comma: 'Let's eat grandpa.' Woops! 'Let's eat, grandpa'

*

2579 US gun law limits personal purchases to one new gun per month; I'm feeling safer

*

2580 if you rent a car and it suffers $5,500 of hail damage — you have to pay for the repairs

*

2581 people who, things that

*

2582 politician objects to a primary school fancy dress event where boys will wear a dress; parents counter the politician's complaint by raising not the $900 target, but $270,000

*

2583 sign on café chalk board: 'Mother-in-law coming

to stay for eight weeks. Purely by coincidence, trading hours will be extended — 6 am to midnight — for the next eight weeks'

2584 text to Ecuador Embassy: 'Room not required for Harry; keep on standby for Andrew'

2585 a leading steak restaurant sings its own praises — but doesn't have hot English mustard

2586 constantly being asked if I want to exit

2587 it pisses me off that after dinner we no longer repair to the study for port

2588 or hoof our way to the top of the peak, and later sojourn at the inn

2589 if a man goes into a forest, speaks his mind, and no one hears, is he still wrong?

*

2590 pleased the surgeon who did my quadruple bypass got a Queen's Birthday honour

*

2591 pleased the abandoned, rat-infested Russian cruise ship Lyubov Orlova, which was found drifting off the coast of Canada, was towed out to sea by the Canadian Coast Guard; reports that monster rats — which had long been eating each other — were seen in their thousands running along the tow rope towards the towing vessel

*

2592 may I please come back as a politician's offspring so I can slip seamlessly into a safe senate seat, get massive superannuation, and take up a major ambassadorship

*

2593 hats off to the major bank which declared it will no longer make loans to mining companies involved in mining fossil fuels — which really pissed off the government

2594 the deaths of so many courageous firefighters and citizens is so terribly sad

2595 I look at the huge (and hugely expensive) ads in the newspaper for a new CEO, and I think, even though I'm old, surely I could do no worse than the recently fired incumbent

2596 mates' rates — something I can say in all honesty I've never experienced

2597 whatever happened to humility, compassion, love and respect?

2598 every 9 minutes an Australian suffers a heart attack

2599 retirement does have its upside; you'll be the first to know when I discover it

2600 six days to pension day; twenty days to the one after that

*

2601 when will all of the corruption, misbehaviour, anger, violence and meanness end?

*

2602 a close friend wrote a book about fifty worthy people, but didn't include me

*

2603 I hope you've been paying attention

*

2604 a lyrebird shifts 155 tonnes of soil and litter in a year

*

2605 foibles which come back to bite you on the bum

*

2606 could have, would have, should have

*

TRULY?

2607 the following people are banned from attending my funeral ...

*

2608 born crying, lived angry, will die disappointed

*

2609 pissed that ABC TV Escape from the City never mentions stamp duty

*

2610 'We're going to need a bigger boat'

*

2611 pissed that we no longer have bodgies and widgies

*

2612 knowing that catbirds chortle, larks warble, hens cackle and sparrows trill

A RAFT OF PISSERS (3)

2613 that a football umpire can't get as honest answer from a player as to whether the latter touched the ball before it went through the goal posts — and has to rely on camera footage

2614 one hundred million Filipinos — and I got Kass

2615 anything which dangles from a car's rear vision mirror; worse if it's fragrant

2616 car stickers which promote Queensland theme parks which I have no interest in ever visiting

2617 people who live on the top floor of our apartment building, who don't send the lift back to the ground floor as a courtesy to the remaining 99% of us

2618 my sons' headmaster once telling me that my elder son was the most polite boy (of 1,400) in his school. I replied, 'Colin, that's really kind of you. However, please don't say another word, because I have an awful feeling it's going to start with "but ..."'

2619 Big Bash cricketer swings and misses twice in a

row. I could do that. Where do I apply, what's the pay, and do bowlers get to use sandpaper?

2620 yet another TV ad where a traditional Aussie dad is portrayed as a loser; giving a 'Dad Talk' to his daughter's grade 6 class, he speaks after a nurse and a pilot, his claim to fame being that he drives a Hilux. Imagine the outrage if the hapless, self-esteem-denied underachiever had been Asian or Middle Eastern — or a mother!

2621 to the Sydney talk back radio host: it's Mitt-sue-bishi, not Mitt-shoe-bishi

2622 surely something is out of whack when a publicly-funded, not-for-profit university has sufficient money to co-sponsor a $71 million sporting competition

2623 when you really (and honestly) ponder it — logically, sensibly, fairly — isn't it the tiniest bit quaint that our head of state isn't a citizen or resident of our Australia?

2624 my cardiologist is going to do something to me this morning and I know not what

2625 so pleased to read that the CEO of my super fund trousered a measly $1.2m last year

2626 calendar quote: 'writers are the engineers of the soul'

2627 US writer Joan Didion: '*A writer is someone who puts words on a page*'

2628 official advice to tourists on a sign in Far North Queensland: 'Try Not To Die'

2629 Simon and Garfunkel: 'People talking without speaking / People hearing without listening'

2630 new local council by-laws determined to make driving my car a thing of the past

2631 losing all of my phone contacts and having to start over, yet again

2632 when my then-wife and I were living in New York, my mother in Melbourne would send us a fax; then, when we got home from work, we'd phone her back, to chat. One day, when we called back, Mum said she was worried her fax machine was about to run out of paper. I told her that wasn't possible because we didn't send faxes to her. *'But,'* she asked, *'doesn't my paper go through to you?'*

2633 TikTok videos which don't show the outcome

2634 the frustrating and infuriating slowness with which drivers move away when the light turns green — after they finish brushing their teeth, fixing their hair, checking their phone

2635 the state Governor holds an afternoon tea to honour people who've given their 100th blood donation; you can tell the blood donors among the crowd because they're the pale ones

2636 for his warm-up in the dressing room prior to

going out to bat, test cricketer great Doug Walters used to throw three darts into a dartboard

2637 the 20-something girl on the tram who constantly sniffed; I asked her if she'd like a tissue, and, well, did all hell break loose?

2638 the (private) high school student who couldn't give the tram driver a simple 'thank you' before she stepped off (great parenting, mum and dad)

2639 people in inconsequential jobs who try to wield power over me

2640 people in consequential jobs who do wield power over me

2641 a survey found the least popular pizza topping in Australia is olives; my money had been on anchovies or pineapple

2642 unbalanced table legs at cafés and restaurants

2643 we pay 3% extra for stuff we buy because feral bogans steal $10 billion worth

2644 the dirty rotten stinking scoundrels at my supermarket who, without warning, have raised the price of tuna by 40 cents a can (15% increase); no warning, no apology, no nothing, just a tiny black label delivering the bad news. Do they think I'm an idiot, or what?

2645 the cruise line which boasts no casinos, no kids; where do I book a room — for life?

2646 the elderly American who sold everything and lived permanently on a cruise ship

2647 survey: '72% of people say they'd save a dog over a stranger'

2648 I've submitted numerous queries to 'Modern Guru' in The Age, but I've never had my question published or my issue addressed, and I'm running out of patience

2649 pissed off by the warm and fuzzy SUV vehicle ads which, when I dig down and discover the true cost, I find the fortnightly payments are more than double my pension

2650 clicking on the 'Contact Us' tab because I want to obtain a real email address, only to get a page of questions and a tiny comments box

2651 drivers in front of me turning left, who wait for the pedestrian besotted with his mobile phone to finish dawdling across the intersection

2652 products which can be purchased only by calling a 1800 number

2653 hundreds of redacted pages in government reports

2654 it shouldn't be forgotten how, in his later years, former PM Malcolm Fraser resigned from the Liberal Party saying it had lost its (liberal) way; sound relevant today?

2655 searching through the rhetoric for policy

2656 wishing politicians would realise that all we punters want to hear is a simple yes or no

2657 last night we watched *Marley And Me*, and when we woke up this morning, Marley had swallowed Kass's wedding ring

2658 people who disavow responsibility for something done because the deed was committed by someone 'above my pay grade'

2659 the waiting is killing me; I'm slowly dying

2660 athletes who (a) never lose it, (b) never stuff up, and (c) have great character

2661 Facebook suggests people who I might like to 'friend'. I feel guilty passing until I realise these very same people could have just as easily friended me, but didn't

2662 the big bash celebrity cricket game to aid bushfire victims was remarkable for the true camaraderie clearly evident among the many athletes from different sporting codes

2663 gender wealth gap as reported: Leonardo Di Caprio, $260 million; Brad Pitt, $300 million; Tom Cruise, $570 million; Nicole Kidman, $129 million

2664 shares skyrocket, shares plummet, shares give back, whatever does that mean?

2665 first names popular among Catholics: Benedict, Maria, Ryan, Jacob, Genevieve, Brenton, Brendon,

Anne-Marie, Bernadette, Dominic, Patrick, George, Xavier

2666 the TV ad for a short-term loan, where the wife knows everything but the clueless husband is nothing short of a total drip; imagine the outcry if the roles were reversed

2667 the other TV ad for a short-term loan, where the clueless husband is strapped to a spinning wheel, and who again comes across as nothing short of a total idiot

2668 every day in Melbourne three cars collide with a tram

2669 twenty-four per cent of Australians don't have children

2670 difficult questions asked by your partner — after she sneaks a glance at your phone

2671 four years ago, we had an opportunity to buy a property in Tasmania; we didn't, and the value of the property has since doubled

2672 I'm told I shouldn't worry about old age because it doesn't last all that long

2673 anxiousness or anxiety; over which should I be more stressed?

2674 it's now official: half of all elderly Australians in aged care are malnourished

2675 fact: you are more likely to be successful if you make your bed each morning

2676 the expert mathematician who, when asked on a TV quiz show how many zeros there are in ten million, froze

2677 the man who designed New York's major roads didn't drive

2678 just asking if a sensible, non-rabid Christian is allowed to work at the ABC?

2679 bushfire smoke at the tennis: *'We'll consider it depending on how it affects the budget'*

2680 too embarrassed to ask what 'double jeopardy laws' are

2681 after waiting for ages in line, being told, *'We don't do that special at this branch'*

2682 okay, allow Chinese to take a 99-year lease on our precious land, but *never to buy it*

2683 a millennial charged his brother $2 for a drumstick ice-cream from his freezer

2684 news report: 'Chinese swimmer out for eight years'; at last, a sporting body with balls

2685 Australians who claim to be Church of England (it went out of existence in 1977)

2686 the eighteen-year-old who sued her parents for having put her in a TV ad as a child

2687 the standard that we walk past is the standard we accept

2688 I'm suffering from gay abandon — and loving every minute of it

2689 praise for big business when it leads social reforms (e.g. plastics waste, climate change, wilderness protection, renewable energy sources, same-sex marriage)

2690 I'm available any time to join a big and potentially lucrative class action

2691 singing falsetto alto in the school choir in year 11 to keep the year eights on note

2692 the incredibly difficult road ahead for young people who identify as non-binary

2693 knowing there are countries where Kass and I could never visit or live safely

2694 being at risk

2695 tears

2696 the terrifying thought as to who would become prime minister if the present incumbent became incapacitated

2697 the number of urinals in a pub is proportional to the number of beer taps in the bars

2698 always on the lookout for the next ATM to ram and rob

2699 I'm keen to hang around to see how things turn out

2700 Fr Rod Bower's church billboards at Gosford always give pause for thought

2701 Trump's mother clearly didn't teach him that being humble means not constantly singing your own praises — and then there is the bit about not lying — 23,000 times

2702 amazing how cooked tomatoes retain so much relative heat

2703 'A horse walks into a bar ...'

2704 vegetables are vegetarians' meat

2705 the purpose of the little toe is to ensure all of the furniture is in its proper place

2706 the correct way to encourage young city unemployed to pick fruit is (a) make fruit picking sexy, (b) hold online seminars to sell sexy fruit picking, (c) pay a sexy wage

2707 why are so many Catholics lapsed?

2708 what would Jesus say about the extraordinary opulence in today's churches?

2709 why, why, why?

2710 I'm told I got phished. WHAT?

2711 conspiracy theories

2712 people who believe conspiracy theories

2713 people who peddle conspiracy theories

2714 people who believe NASA's space program, including the 1969 moon landing, is fake

2715 why doesn't today's newspaper give tomorrow's winning lotto numbers?

2716 why didn't today's newspaper run my piece after it promised it would

2717 my headmaster wrote in his autobiography that to be a good school teacher you have to like the little swines

2718 never thought I'd love a set of recliner chairs as much as I do the one we have now

2719 when life sucks like never before and I no longer wish to be part of it

2720 people who run hot and cold on their football team

2721 I'm running hot and cold on my football team

2722 'epic' is used way too often

2723 'iconic' is used way too often

2724 'heroic' is used way too often

2725 'unprecedented' is used way too often

2726 'unique' is used way too often

2727 'very unique' is an oxymoron; it's either unique or it's not

2728 'way too often' is used way too often

2729 people who refinance their home loan for short-term gain

2730 a dumb politician challenging for the party leadership usually means he's courageous

2731 'courageous' in politics usually means foolish

2732 the bogan tennis player who said, 'All I do is count my money, count my millions'

2733 tennis players whose mothers cringe over their son's dreadful behaviour

2734 Venus is the only planet which rotates clockwise

2735 Chris Scott, Geelong Cats coach: 'The problem with kicking a goal against the West Coast Eagles is the ball then has to go back to the centre'

2736 an all-indigenous Northern Territory AFL team ('The People's Team')

2737 crowdfunding an all-indigenous Northern Territory AFL team ('The People's Team')

2738 tens of thousands of Aussies would contribute funds to an all-indigenous Northern Territory AFL team ('The People's Team')

2739 when you really think about it, eating meat is pretty damn gross

2740 28% of people are virgins when they marry

2741 motor racing still includes the ridiculous, childish post-race spraying of champagne

2742 I'd like to know the profit margins promised by business brokers to prospective aged care facility investors — and the average daily meal allowance per resident

2743 strategies used by aged care providers to improve

profit margins (e.g. screwing down resident/staff ratios, daily meal allowances)

2744 announcement from Buckingham Palace: *'Better days will return'*

2745 Prince Charles: *'You Victorians are made of tough stuff'*

2746 the prime number immediately preceding 29 is…?

2747 2020 can go and get f***ed

2748 grateful for the colour in my life

2749 grateful for the flowers in my life

2750 grateful for having Kass in my life

2751 disappointed I haven't done better in life

2752 inspired to write more

2753 inspired to write better

2754 inspired to be more adventurous with my writing

2755 inspired to walk more — within reason, of course

2756 if you hold down the '0' key and swipe left you will get the degrees symbol

2757 I have 100 followers on Twitter, yeh!

2758 when this book comes out, I hope to get many more followers on Twitter

2759 sparkling wine is waiting in the fridge for when this book comes out

2760 a senior journalist just tweeted 'practise' as a noun

2761 58% of people admit to having taken an illegal 'sickie'

2762 millennials who cashed in their allowed $20,000 super—and used it on gambling—ought to be made to attend a workshop on responsible personal financial management

2763 only 7% of women trust their men to do the laundry correctly

2764 the prohibitive cost of Pay TV (thus being unable to watch all footy) is something for which thousands of fans will never forgive the AFL

2765 international cricket gradually being switched to Pay TV only

2766 the New York couple which bought a farm in Portugal cut open the huge heavy welded shut doors to discover they now owned fifty priceless vintage cars

2767 you phone the bank, and instead of hearing a human say 'hello' you get the pre-recorded bank's life history — delivered by Kass's cousin in Manila

2768 a study finds baby boomers stay in a job for 6.8 years; millennials, 2.8 years

2769 a major company's board chair says millennials are 'hug-dependent, thank-you-seeking marshmallows'

2770 Michael to Kass: *'Why do you love me so much?'* Kass: *'Do I have a choice?'*

2771 all things preposterous

2772 we have a gin distillery within walking distance of our home; pack the sandwiches

2773 two-thirds of drivers speed up at a yellow light

2774 radio 3AW has begun to schedule additional ads after the start and before the finish of news breaks; as if there weren't enough ads already

2775 Pope Francis once worked as a bouncer in a nightclub

2776 can the American FBI extradite a member of the British Royal Family?

2777 people on average keep thirteen secrets

2778 I just discovered that the gripe meant for this number was a repeat; sorry

2779 regarding the Great Wall of China, I've never really understood why they bothered

2780 7% of people say they would kill someone for $10,000,000

2781 Kevin, the boy in Home Alone, is now forty

2782 I wrote to a friend in prison

2783 my friend in prison wrote back to me

2784 downright stupid, bogan mullet haircuts

2785 character is destiny

2786 owning up when I'm undercharged — or given too much change

2787 sometimes not owning up when I'm undercharged — or given too much change

2788 I was told I only needed to wear a mask when I went shopping, but when I got to the shops everyone was also wearing clothes

2789 I was lonely until I glued a coffee cup to my car's roof; now everyone waves at me

2790 Forbes says Australia is the eighteenth smartest country in the world, just ahead of Taiwan, Austria, Finland, Hungary and Denmark; Japan is top; the US is fourth on the list

2791 pandemonium on Sweden's roads the day in 1967 it switched from driving on the left to driving on the right

2792 the woman who drops a coin into the guy's coffee mug, thinking he's homeless

2793 two more TV ads where the woman is on the front foot, organises the couple's insurance policy, while the dumb male looks on with a vacant smile

2794 again, in a TV ad, the man is made to look so freaking stupid?

2795 five millennials are bushwalking, but they pause to watch a horse race on a phone; would five millennials really do that? Honestly?

2796 Kass says that instead of writing, I should go online to suss out aged care facilities

2797 'Well may you ask, Matty, but I couldn't possibly comment on that'

2798 two losses and the coach has the club board's full support; four losses and questions are being asked; six losses and the coach wants to spend more time with his family

2799 are we going to blindly follow the US into war in the South China Sea — or will someone grow a brain?

2800 thirteen days until my next pension payment

2801 Joe Blakes on land; Noah's Arks in water — I'm allergic to both

2802 the Australian Medical Association seems to have a new president every other day

2803 out of whisky (again)

2804 yesterday, I had a Barry Crocker of a day

2805 often, I wish I'd been born indigenous, been blessed with loving parents who ensured I had a good education, and spent my life fighting hard for my people

2806 the private sector might be the best to build growth in the economy, but can business be trusted to not distribute all of that growth to itself (i.e. as bonuses to its executives)?

2807 Australia is drifting towards Indonesia at the rate of six inches every 100 years; yikes!

2808 apologies to all the decent Karens

2809 apologies to all the decent Kevins

2810 *'You had me at "Hello"'*

2811 *'That'll do, Pig, that'll do'*

2812 we were watching Big Brother — and Kass said she'd vote me out

2813 I'm not a poet and I know it

2814 advice to male boomers: never trust a fart, never walk past a urinal, never waste an erection

2815 researchers are making more powerful and longer lasting tear gas

2816 200,000 Victorians admit to driving without wearing a seat belt

2817 I keep telling Kass it's our week for Powerball

2818 major bank to teach ethics to its employees, from top down; goodness gracious

2819 the BBC radio journalist who just said 'interestink'

2820 can we get rid of 'basically', 'so' and 'um'' especially from people who work in universities and who should know a whole lot better — and who talk on radio and TV?

2821 did you spend the $750 x 2 pensioner supplement payments or, like me, did you put the money in the bank for a future rainy day?

2822 there are 43,000 people in jail in Australia

2823 facetious contains all five vowels in alphabetical order

2824 only one in 1,000 manuscripts gets published

2825 Sir Winston Churchill: *'Never give in, never give in; never, never, never, never'*

2826 pity the poor dolts who took up the government coronavirus bonus to cash in $20,000 of their superannuation to pay household bills, only to blow the whole damn lot on online gambling

2827 not knowing when to remain silent, and when to let all hell rip

2828 gambling on Russian ping pong

2829 report: more than one-third of Australians are racist; denying it won't change the fact

2830 Australia Post should send every child, aged 5–15, five pieces of note paper, five envelopes and five stamps, plus fun hints on how to write a catchy letter to someone special

2831 I can run the OECD for a $399,000 tax-free salary which comes with twelve staff; sign me up — immediately

2832 going into a teenager's bedroom is like going into IKEA. You go in just to have a look, and you come out with six plates, three cups, four bowls and a set of cutlery

2833 wishing the PM would frown instead of smirk, and drop that arrogant, supercilious look; frowning shows empathy and vulnerability, something people need and want in their leader in stressful times (ask the masterful John Howard)

2834 no cars on the road tonight but I saw seventeen bikes/motorbikes delivering meals

2835 love my early morning scrolls through Twitter blocking gambling outlets

2836 blocking annoying tweeters

2837 advertisements promoting Big Brother cite meanness as a key program feature — charming lessons for children

2838 young people might do well to save rather than spend all of their wages on Friday/Saturday boozy nights out; drive past a night venue to see them for yourself

2839 young people want it all, they want it easy and they want it now

2840 Roy Slaven, 'Bludging on the Blind Side' podcast: *'The good thing about reducing the number of rugby umpires from two to one is only one car will get torched after the game!'*

2841 falling from grace

2842 the pent-up anxiety which comes from waiting, waiting, waiting for surgery

2843 young workers (especially) who are employed as 'independent contractors' and denied basic 'employee' entitlements like super, annual and sick leave, travel allowances, etc.

2844 close inspection confirms no amount of wealth guarantees good looks

2845 doctors identify themselves by subtly wearing a stethoscope; I not-too-subtly wear my Centrelink number

2846 how many boomers upon retiring use their superannuation to buy a motorhome instead of putting it into an interest-bearing pension fund?

2847 TripAdvisor says there are 276 cafés/restaurants in our suburb; I don't believe it

2848 because I was treated so shabbily at rowing at school, I declare it to be the sport closest to watching grass grow

2849 ex-Hawthorn player/captain/coach John Kennedy Snr's famous three-quarter time address to his players: 'DO SOMETHING!'

2850 only 9% of Australian authors earn more than $40,000 per year

2851 the TV show has 'New' in its title but we all know they are showing reruns

2852 radio, long considered the most intimate broadcast medium, is being challenged by podcasts

2853 sad that no one ever calls me 'Petal'; the closest I get is 'Sunshine'

2854 idea: footballers' renumeration henceforth to be

$1,500 per possession, coaches to get $40,000 per game won; would that improve the game?

2855 Liberal candidate for Eden-Monaro by-election defied 65% local poll result in 2017 and voted against same-sex marriage; under which rock does this mob find its candidates?

2856 how long is it fair to wait for a reply to two polite, non-offensive emails before I'm allowed to spit the dummy and call the person who didn't respond a miserable piece of poo?

2857 asking the miserable piece of poo referred to above to choose which gripe on this page refers to her

2858 when it's their turn

2859 my grandmother never learned to work the washing machine; her husband did the washing

2860 loath to leave the safety of home for a road trip — for fear of being met with harm

2861 I get it that a TV ad featuring a couple standing in a swimming pool, farting, gets your attention, but does it make you want to buy the product they are trying to sell? Hardly

2862 Trump supporter in Texas threatened shoppers with a chainsaw

2863 can't wait to scan the Queen's Birthday Honours List to see what I've won

2864 since when did 'in the future' become 'going forward?'

2865 apparently in some religions you pray to different gods for different things: one god for good health and another god for a Mercedes Benz

2866 we had to talk about Trump

2867 we had to talk about Pence

2868 we had to talk about McConnell

2869 we had to talk about all of the Republicans who knew they should have spoken up, but didn't have the guts to do so

2870 Australian universities sitting on $20 billion in cash reserves, crying poor, putting off staff, yet calling for greater government funding

2871 think of the poor old folk who received a threatening robodebt letter wrongly demanding repayment of a huge sum — and in despair and fear took their life before the error was corrected

2872 the best way to earn endearment and loyalty of grandchildren is to make the parents (in the middle) the common enemy

2873 is taking a wee in the shower really a jail-able offence?

2874 3.3% of Australia's population is indigenous; 28% of people in jail in Australia are indigenous; figure that one out

2875 there have been 434 black deaths in custody since the royal commission into black deaths in custody, in 1991

2876 indigenous Australians are sick and tired of being sick and tired — and living in fear

2877 people who say 'less is more' usually have nothing useful to say

2878 will the Chinese govt ban AFL games being played there; I fervently hope so

2879 excuse me, but how many times did the now prime minister vote against a banking royal commission; was it twenty-six times?

2880 my nephew in the Philippines was quoted a $400 'registration' fee to apply for a job on a cruise ship — another cruise line assured me charging a registration fee for employment is not normal industry practice

2881 still feeling maudlin and melancholy over the death of our younger son; forever will

2882 why don't parking meters give credit for time unused? After all, the machines have the technological capacity

2883 it's cute how National Party members manage to get their leader's name into every question they ask in Parliamentary Question Time, but Liberal members don't mention him when they ask a question

2884 I miss reading the phone book

2885 a father pulled his sons from junior football after AFL teams 'took a knee' in support of Black Lives Matter; a St Kilda fan requested a membership refund for the same reason

2886 I'm even more convinced I should have my own, prime-time talk show

2887 the best place to hide is closest to the flame

2888 Australian Christian Lobby declares the Black Lives Matter movement the anti-Christ

2889 millions of Australians don't give a fig about knowing our country's sorry history; all they care about is who won Masterchef

2890 current status of political parties: Labor — corrupt; Liberal — heartless; Greens — looney; One Nation — imbecilic; Derryn Hinch — tick

2891 Sydney parking inspectors denied an annual pay increase if they fail to meet their quota of 21 fines issued per shift

2892 I've just realised so many people will still be alive after I die

2893 Channel 10 wins The Bogan Stakes

2894 my son sings and plays keyboard and trumpet online on Tuesday and Friday nights at 8.30 pm AEST at http://twitch.tv/richardthornton

2895 Australia has 900 forklift accidents a year, and a TV ad has a forklift driver looking sideways — not straight ahead — as he drives past a group of workers (totally irresponsible)

2896 if you put too much emphasis on age it begins to affect you

2897 who was the bright spark who decided to put the Kmart checkout machines in the middle of the store?

2898 dogs have owners, cats have servants

2899 what in heaven's name is planking?

2900 Kass wants a baby

2901 I was at agricultural college in 1973 when Britain joined the European Communities; Australia's agricultural trade was decimated; 43 years later, post-Brexit, a return to free trade is on the cards. Negotiate damn hard, I say, and teach the poms a lesson they won't forget

2902 pissed that I cannot solve today's Sudoku and nine-letter-word puzzles

2903 another TV ad where an older woman cyclist has all the knowledge about life insurance, while her husband's contribution to the discussion is to make a lame joke; imagine the outcry of sexism if the roles were reversed and the woman was the idiot

2904 can I buy real estate in China?

2905 ABC TV Insiders host David Speers to Labor guest Chris Bowen: 'So, a little bit of branch stacking is okay, then?'

2906 Trump said he'd been talking to hundreds of state governors: excuse me, there are fifty states, fifty governors

2907 300 trekkers have died climbing Mt Everest

2908 Trump: *'When you do testing to that extent, you are going to find many more cases. So I said to my people, "slow the testing, slow the testing."'* WHAT?

2909 extremism

2910 delinquency

2911 lunacy

2912 how can a weedicide get a political 'nothing to see here' tick here in Australia, but in the USA the same product is forced to pay damages of $15.8 billion?

2913 when are TV reality shows going to realise 20% of people are gay, and include them?

2914 one of my mother's friends said her (adult) children had gone around her home putting their name labels on the underside of all her furniture (in readiness for their inheritance)

2915 elder abuse is largely hidden but common enough for the government to run TV ads calling it out

2916 airline official: *'We've had flights with more dogs on board than people'*

2917 I've not read one Dicey Topics (Good Weekend magazine in The Age) interview where the subject has said she or he couldn't live without God

2918 our balcony plants are officially cactus

2919 Me: 'What are you doing, Kass?' Kass: 'Why is it any of your business?'

2920 why does everything begin to go downhill once the day begins?

2921 why are we here?

2922 Leonard Cohen's answer to the meaning of Life: 'Do doo dum dum'

2923 to be or not to be a show jumper, that's the equestrian

2924 there are over 300 different jobs from which to choose in Australia's Defence Forces

2925 I appreciate many media outlets want me to subscribe, but the fact is I can get all the news and commentary I want from free-to-air TV, radio, free print media and free podcasts

2926 I value my private health insurance for ancillary services, but I would never bother with hospital cover after having received four days of exceptional care in a public hospital

2927 there are 1.13 million boats in the UK

2928 Kass has her permanent residency; all she needs now is her citizenship and Aussie passport; what a lucky country we are (as long as we avoid Brunei)

2929 unlikely to be able to visit Kass's elderly parents in the Philippines until at least the middle of 2021

2930 how good is it that the captain and coach of the Storm visited the Warriors rooms post-game to give them encouragement after their huge loss

2931 19 is a prime number; it is also the age I lost my virginity

2932 ABC *Songs of Praise* lauds Captain Cook as a man of enormous integrity. Hmm, tell that to indigenous Aussies

2933 American showman PT Barnum: *'I don't give a damn what you say about me as long as you spell my name right'*

2934 CEO who gets $65,000 a day sacks 6,000 employees because his company … 'cannot afford them'

2935 which of these should take precedence: public health, civil liberties or the economy?

2936 England voted for Colombia (against Australia/NZ) to host the 2023 Women's World (soccer) Cup; bear that in mind when the mongrel poms arrive here (put them up in kennels)

2937 when I was born in 1949, Ben Chifley was Australia's prime minister, Clement Attlee was UK prime minister, and Harry Truman was US president; I feel thoroughly antique

2938 inconsiderate residents who treat our apartments' foyer — right outside our door — as a conference venue

2939 TV coverage of lawn bowls would be much enhanced if cameras were attached to the bowls

2940 $500 million to enhance an already adequate and respectful Australian War Memorial

2941 tigers have striped skin, not just striped fur

2942 looking for a property developer or generous Chinese infiltrator with whom I can become best friends

2943 wow, that was close; I nearly divulged a life secret

2944 people shouldn't have to go to *A Current Affair* or talkback radio to get an injustice rectified

2945 my mother asked a friend to co-sponsor a mutual friend's nomination for membership of a posh golf club. In her *confidential* letter of 'support', the woman wrote, 'I don't see why Betty shouldn't be a member of the club, but then again I don't see why she should be.' Mum was furious. I told her it was not her place to open the envelope addressed to the club secretary, and it served her right for opening and reading the letter

2946 how about *Farmer Wants a Husband* with two men attracted to each other

2947 Sir Winston Churchill: *'When you walk through hell it is best that you keep walking'*

2948 who is more employable in 2021: a 50-year-old with three masters' degrees or a 25 year-old with a trade certificate?

2949 our days are numbered

2950 Six per cent of university students admit to cheating at exams; 8% admit to taking an exam for someone else (usually with money paid to a 'professional' agency)

2951 if we win Powerball, Kass wants every child in the Philippines to have school shoes; I want every child in Australia to have a school uniform, school shoes, school bag, and lunch

2952 idea: establish a non-profit Eminent People's Council excluding rabid left/right ideological zealots to appraise and comment on public issues on behalf of middle-ground Australians (remit to include calling out lies, corruption and sheer bad/unfair policy)

2953 I get to choose who goes on the Eminent People's Council

2954 the world's richest 380 people have more than the bottom half of the planet, combined

2955 a US writer received 336 rejections before first being published; her advice to other would-be authors: *'keep writing'*

2956 Margaret Mitchell received thirty-eight rejections before 'Gone with the Wind' was published

2957 the Australian Constitution allows for New Zealand to become a state; why on earth would New Zealanders want to do that?

2958 when you cut into a cooked chicken — and it's pink inside

2959 give jobseekers too much support and they might not look for work; give them too little support and they might not be alive to look for work

2960 why didn't one of our multi-billionaires buy Virgin Airways?

2961 sign outside our local pub: 'If you're thirsty, come in; if you aren't, keep driving'

2962 QLD premier: *'The border between Queensland and Victoria will remain closed;'* excuse me, exactly which border is that?

2963 press release: 'Australia and New Zealand to amalgamate their defence forces'

2964 imagine the public outcry if the IQs of Homer and Marge Simpson were reversed

2965 1,700,000 lovers of the ABC should each be asked to give $50 to an ABC GoFundMe page to repair the $85m deficit

2966 Einstein: *'I know not the weapons that World War III will be fought with, but World War IV will be fought with sticks and stones'*

2967 bottle of Grange Hermitage sells for $103,000

2968 do you think city born-and-bred prospective brides on *Farmer wants a Wife* have any idea how lonely life on a broad acre wheat farm can be, where the bloke spends more time talking to and nurturing his tractor, than to and with her?

2969 it took a respected AFL coach to get a no brainer umpiring malpractice rectified — players who hug the ball instead of disposing of it, now get pinged (or supposedly so)

2970 Tasmania to re-enter the National Basketball League

2971 the year before our school's annual marathon, a boy collapsed, so the next year our event was reduced from 24 to 21 miles; then in our year the headmaster's son collapsed, so the run was reduced again, this time to 17 miles; today it is 23 km (14 miles)

2972 Twitter informs or Twitter offends — you decide!

2973 two university professors co-authoring a piece in The Age drop two English clangers in the space of four lines; it's not 'those that refuse', it's 'those who refuse'; it's not 'have both taken', it's 'both have taken'

2974 Virgin Airlines creditor demands the return of four jet engines leased to the airline; tell them to pop around after lunch and we'll have them ready

2975 some people are amazingly connected to what they do well, others aren't

2976 and there I was absolutely sure that Obama would take Secretary of State

2977 wrong calls

2978 Kass agonising over which earrings to wear to the nail parlour

2979 still cannot fathom how monstrously tall buildings stay up (I am so scared of them)

2980 Kass looking stunning with the earrings she chose to wear to the nail shop

2981 sometimes I think I'm hyperactive, manic, bipolar; other times I think I'm just brilliant

2982 when we're almost there, but not quite

2983 people who feign embarrassment and shyness at being painted, but actually relish it

2984 when will we have the long-promised federal anti-corruption body?

2985 it's been seven years since I walked 543 km of the Spanish Camino's 800 km; I so wish I could do it again, this time with Kass, but I fear it's now beyond my ageing body

2986 if only I knew back then what I know now

2987 I can't recall ever having received a spray, but by golly, I know I've given a few

2988 the sense of accomplishment when one successfully undertakes a speeding tram

2989 a reality TV program with a convicted drug smuggler as a contestant; really?

2990 beguiled

2991 seduced

2992 seduced again

2993 overlooked

2994 forgotten

2995 wanting to witness more things pretty

2996 my $20 sweater cost $12.50 to dry clean

2997 the faster and louder the American spruiks his get rich scheme, the dodgier he comes across

2998 and here was I thinking 'happy ending' was a tear-jerker of a movie

2999 teacher to student: 'Where to after school?' Boy: 'Onto dad's farm.' Teacher: 'What as, fertiliser?'

3000 the University of Tasmania hosted a panel discussion on 'Stay or go?' (to the mainland, where greater opportunity beckons) — courageous of them to raise the ever-present elephant in the Tasmanian room

3001 reports Trump wanted his image added to Mount Rushmore

3002 Trump disembowelling the US Postal Service to reduce the number of postal votes (which tend to favour Democrats)

3003 30% of people admit to having shoplifted at least once in their life

3004 it's not home schooling, people, it's distance learning

3005 when I feel inadequate

3006 Kass threatening to install hand rails for me

3007 TikTok is telling me how to do something cool on my iPhone, but when I try to do what they say, the menu item is not there

3008 research shows 35% of people have extramarital fantasies

3009 I tick so many boxes

3010 so petulant when a FB friend doesn't let you look at his/her list of friends

3011 can we have another update on what the locked-up Sri Lankan family is costing us?

3012 deciding which of my least dirty clothes to wear today

3013 cricket formats are now defined by the colour of the ball — red, white or pink (WTF?)

3014 Donald Trump interview with Australian journalist Jonathan Swan was far better than the 1977 fireside chats which David Frost did with Richard Nixon

3015 the university student studying maths is unable to recite the alphabet

3016 France and Britain have twice considered becoming one country (in 1940 and 1956)

3017 the aged care resident (one day, me) who, every morning, says, '*Damn, I've woken up*'

3018 received confirmation today from the hospital that I'm on the list for surgery to remove part of my bowel; a cheery prospect, especially given what the worst will mean

3019 yikes! (a colostomy bag!)

3020 my school's biannual magazine, devoted primarily to news of fellow alumni, has arrived; again I quickly checked that I wasn't included in the Vale section

3021 you can smell only so many roses

3022 much to my shame I too was initially against the mother when the dingo took the baby — and I'm still feeling guilty about it (as are millions of other, fair-minded Australians)

3023 prediction: many of the two million Australians who 'negatively-gear' an investment property are going to suffer a massive blow in 2021, when interest rates go up and values fall

3024 I don't do 'negative-gearing,' never have, never will, and not jealous of those who do

3025 exactly what are franking credits?

3026 thinking of three people who sadly let their lives end far too soon, for no good reason

3027 I've told Kass what I want in the eulogy; her last words to be: 'Michael said he left the money under ...'

3028 life is but a dream

3029 death

3030 never leave dying so late there'll be no one left to attend your funeral

3031 Eighty-two per cent of people believe in an afterlife

3032 everything will be tickety-boo, if that's not double Dutch to you

3033 the nastiness and pettiness behind confiscating the phones of refugees in detention, especially the Sri Lankan family stuck on Christmas Island

3034 regarding climate change deniers: I repeat, show them how to make money from it and they'll soon come on board

3035 anti-vaxxers

3036 anyone who isn't in the silent majority

3037 ants crawling out of an open wound in a resident in an aged care facility

3038 when the gift you're given comes without the necessary batteries

3039 millennials accusing baby boomers of not caring about climate change because we won't be around to suffer its effects, yet we sensible boomers worry constantly about it

3040 when you find you're speaking to the monkey and not the organ grinder

3041 politicians who say, *'I don't hold a hose!'* (I don't fight fires)

3042 back when AI used to mean artificial insemination

3043 ignoramuses

3044 that I spent three years as boarding housemaster to 120 teenage boys (always trying to reason with them), but didn't know until years later that the human brain doesn't fully develop until the age twenty-six

3045 the two gamblers who lost $60,000 and $45,000 respectively on a football match clearly didn't know that you never ever bet on anything that can talk

3046 a shearer gets paid $3.19 per sheep; a barber charges ten times that to cut a human head of hair (shearers on average shear one hundred sheep per day)

3047 'If it's not on, it's not on' used to refer to condoms; today it's about face masks

3048 it's hard, when Carlton plays Collingwood, to work out the lesser of two evils

3049 Eddie Betts to a team mate who's about to kick for goal: *'Give it to a goal kicker!'*

3050 never a worse time to try to sell a stable of magazine mastheads (millions lost!)

3051 never a worse time to have a significant birthday

3052 never a worse time to die

3053 'Happy Holidays' when the word is Christmas

3054 ignorant bogans who call it daylight savings (plural)

3055 *'We've had many learnings ...'* – the word is lessons

3056 'I want' never gets

3057 films which leave me anxious and afraid'

3058 why are people who look after money paid significantly more than people who look after people?

3059 footballers no longer are dropped; they are 'managed'

3060 does anyone on TV's *Home and Away* ever actually *do anything*?

3061 guilty as charged of being a cheapskate: for my birthday my daughter gave me a $60 bottle of whisky; for her birthday I gave her a $16 bottle of Irish Cream

3062 all I want for Father's Day is a cherry ripe and a scratchy

3063 horse racing speak: *'She come out and done good'*

3064 in 1987, Kerry Packer sold Channel Nine to Alan Bond for $1 billion; three years later he bought it back for half that amount

3065 'The Block Kitchen Reveals' — can you think of anything more mind-numbing?

3066 *'The wine was full-bodied, nuanced, and with a hint of purple.'* WHAT?

3067 when the grandchildren ask, 'Are we there yet?'

3068 when the adult children ask, 'Are we there yet?'

3069 when Kass asks, 'Are we there yet?'

3070 when a private school principal says, 'The class

of 2020 *have* (has) *managed more change than any who (which) have* (has) *come before them* (it).'

3071 unsolicited phone surveys from people who won't go away (and even those who will)

3072 I'm well and truly over being age-shamed

3073 evildoers cannot be identified 'for legal reasons'; what's all that about?

3074 the TV ad where the business woman takes a work Zoom call in her bedroom, but there in the bed behind her trying to hide is young Tim from Finance. Did someone say KFC?

3075 nothing remotely equals happy hour

3076 would our quarterly body corporate fees be less if the communications manager didn't have to send a second email correcting her mistake in her first email?

3077 Prince William: *'You are the people which'*; people are who, things are which – and to think that one day he is going to be your king (not mine; I'll be dead)

3078 one-quarter of Australians have less than $1,000 in savings

3079 the world sends half a million text messages every second (guilty as charged, Your Honour)

3080 people with famous connections: me, I sat on the same toilet seat after a politician

3081 really disappointed that The Naked Chef turned out to be a show about cooking

3082 the BCF ad where the dad knocks his son out of the boat — another typical Aussie male battler made out to be a total dumb-arse

3083 anything that's wicked is worth a second glance

3084 mental health: a top cricketer struggles to swap the gas bottles on the barbecue; I cried my eyes out when I couldn't locate a recently paid annual rates bill

3085 it's the vibe, that's what it is

3086 what in God's name are 'carry over credits', or am I a complete dumb-arse (again)

3087 so many senior positions for which I am perfectly suited advertised in the paper: chief of staff to the lord mayor, manager of community relations at the City of Frankston, CEO of the Cohuna Hospital; do they all offer wheelchair access?

3088 being published is so much better than winning lotto — even if the odds are far less attractive

3089 a contestant on The Chase says if she won money she would hire a stretch limo for her son's upcoming nuptials; such a wise and prudent and responsible mum

3090 'increasinkly' (podcaster), 'sayink' (radio host), 'battink' (cricket commentator)

3091 if a non-resident, non-citizen can be Queen of Australia, then surely I can be King of New Zealand

3092 time to pardon AngusFromTownHall,

BridgetFromSportsFunding, StuartFromRobodebt, RichardFromAgedCare and JoshFromAccounts

3093 furious readers

3094 the time I was early for a book signing — so I signed copies of a friend's book for him

3095 amazing how satellite dishes which look for intelligent life always face away from earth

3096 when you realise you're swimming outside the flags

3097 whoops! I just friended someone who works for the NZ National Party; now I feel like I've betrayed Jacinda — out future PM

3098 Santa once was green. The red Santa with black belt and white hair was created by Coca-Cola

3099 asking a woman to reverse a car and trailer is like asking a man to knit

3100 still pissed how as a 17-year-old jackaroo I was paid $9 a week, plus all I could eat

3101 what's the point of giving the team a pep talk if the players go out and score 6 for 8?

3102 after seventy-one years I've discovered red wine doesn't make tooth ache any worse

3103 for goodness sake, Channel 7; 'Australia needs 90 runs to win,' not need. A collective noun is singular; get it right for the sake of our collective grandchildren

3104 a weekly real estate magazine is read by a million

people, but there's only 58 properties from which to choose

3105 what else possibly could go wrong in the world in 2021, especially at Christmas? Announcement from stable: 'It's a GIRL!'

3106 lobsters have claws, crayfish don't

3107 anything which, or anyone who, might be described as a slippery little sucker

3108 schmoozing invariably leads to trouble

3109 given up trying to chew beef

3110 given up trying to understand or even hear the lyrics to today's excuse for music

3111 worried my remaining teeth will splinter on yoghurt

3112 people who change their mind — for the worse

3113 terrified someone will propose charades on Christmas Day

3114 would I want to own an NBA team? Nah!

3115 but then, again, if it meant I'd forever be surrounded by a million sycophants fulfilling my every wish, maybe I would reconsider and give it a go

3116 if they didn't want the stiff penalties and ruined reputations (assuming they enjoyed good reputations in the first place), they never should have knocked down the historic Carlton pub

3117 the dog ate my homework

3118 the dog ate my list of passwords

3119 the best thing about grand-parenting is … being able to hand them back

3120 the best thing about visiting the grandchildren is probably the coffee

3121 recently, my son (forty-two and father of three) took me aside, and said, *'Dad, I want to thank you.'* 'What for? I asked. *'I now know how much work is involved in being a parent, and I want to thank you because we three must have been right little shits!'* I replied, *'You were!'*

3122 Kass cooking dinner and me drinking a glass or two of whisky; a fair distribution of work tasks, I believe

3123 my bad

3124 time to pull the plug completely on China

3125 how come the more self-promotion the cricketing elites do on TV — ads saying how good they all are — the more my mind jumps to Sandpapergate

3126 fingers crossed I'll get a call-up in the next cabinet reshuffle

3127 morons who dice with death surfing in unprecedented, hugely dangerous seas

3128 kids playing in the shallows in five-feet-high foam, and their parents sitting back on the sand, laughing; how quickly could one of those kids fall over into the foam and never be seen again

3129 human fruitcakes

3130 my Yorkshire-born grandfather called me a duffer; I told him I'd never stolen a single head of cattle in my life

3131 people who post impossible number puzzles on FB

3132 people who disclose the answers to impossible number puzzles on FB

3133 why are actors so short?

3134 wishing I could find Boris Johnson's letter

3135 Sir Ken Robinson's 2006 Ted Talk: '*The purpose of our body is to transport our head to the next meeting*'

3136 spreading ashes would have to be the most macabre of all human pursuits; I want my ashes thrown out with the garbage

3137 there is something pleasing, therapeutic even, about using government (pension) money to buy a bottle of whisky

3138 big tick to Coles for its Boston bun ($3.50) and its crusty Vienna loaf ($2.50)

3139 cricket commentator describing an umpire: '*He's a man who doesn't speak unless he can improve on silence*'

3140 AFL stars dine with a 'person of interest' to police; will footballers never learn?

3141 I've never understood how you can say you're a Christian and worship money

3142 the terrifying moment when you casually think

about a product — and straight away an ad for it pops up on your phone: creepy! I forced my brain to think 'sex' and an ad for male enhancement formula suddenly danced onto my screen

3143 editrix

3144 I've often wondered how much money and threats of disendorsement are needed to keep a politician in line

3145 news report: *'Victoria is humiliated that it took a NSW public inquiry to discover money laundering going on at a gaming venue at 8 Whiteman Street, Melbourne.'*

3146 Papua New Guinea signs a Belt and Road Initiative agreement with China — for a fishing industrial park on Daru Island — 200 km from Australia!

3147 people encouraged to refinance their mortgage, when I want to refinance my life

3148 we just bought a new mattress — but we forgot to ask for the steak knives

3149 are we allowed yet to get on the beers?

3150 still regret that I never took, or was allowed to take, piano lessons, or learned to sing

ACE ENGINEER

3151 At agricultural college, we had just one oral exam. As opposed to a written one. The subject was agricultural engineering, my worst subject by far. Motors and I have never seen eye to eye. The lecturer in charge of the subject, Alan, was a nice enough bloke; often, we would drink together at the local pub. But come exam time it was a whole other story. The moment of truth in the exam came when Alan held up what to me looked like a small flying saucer, a metal thingy which fitted neatly in the palm of his hand. Turning the object over, he asked me which way up in the tractor it went. I replied that if he told me what the cute thing was, I'd have a guess. Failed.

CAUGHT SHORT

I still think of a certain event at boarding school — and what might have been!

3152 At boarding school, we had a much revered yet feared headmaster. We also had an unspoken law that when sitting on the toilet you kept the cubicle door open. (There is a connection coming.) If you were found sitting in a cubicle with the door closed, it was obligatory to have a bucket of water thrown over the door onto you. One day, the headmaster was caught short on his walk home and rushed to use the toilet in our boarding house. Naturally, being the headmaster, he had the door shut. A boy went in, saw pants down under the 'half' door, and rushed off to fetch a pail of water. Upon returning with bucket in hand, but before tipping the contents over the occupant of the stall, the boy called out, 'So, who's this smart bastard?' Whereupon the headmaster, in his superbly rich and distinguishable voice, boomed from inside the stall, 'I *might be smart, but I'm definitely NOT a bastard.*' In a flash, the boy dropped the bucket and ran for his life. Imagine the hullabaloo if the boy had drenched the headmaster. That he didn't achieve his goal pissed off all of us.

LETTING GO

3153 I was in my forties and been experiencing tough times, financially. Because things were tight, as a consequence, I decided to sell my boyhood model railway set. It caused me enormous pain, as if I was cutting off my right ear. I'd had the collection since I was six. My kids weren't at all concerned that I planned to sell, but to me, the trains, carriages, tunnels and signal boxes were beyond precious. I called a dealer, and we met outdoors. My sadness was obvious, and it prompted him to offer me a terribly low and unfair price. But I needed the cash, and reluctantly, I succumbed, helping to transfer the five boxes into his car's boot. I cried all the way home for having lost my beloved train set. I was more than pissed off.

JONATHON

Pre-coronavirus, I heard two successive ministers for aged care say 40 per cent of elderly in nursing homes have no visitors — no family, no friends, no one! It pissed me off, enormously.

3154 It prompted me to join an official visitor program. My thinking was to try to lessen the loneliness for just one person. Following an interview and training video, I was matched with a 91-year-old gentleman in a care facility not far from my home. I was full of apprehension. What if Jonathon and I weren't a suitable match? If we weren't, how would I manage a whole hour with him each Wednesday? How was Jonathon, mentally? Was dementia an issue? If so, how would I cope? As it turned out, my worrying was unwarranted. Jonathon and I hit it off brilliantly from the outset. A friend of actors Michael Caine and Terence Stamp, Jonathon had been brought to Australia by Crawford Productions in the 1960s, to write scripts for 'Homicide',

'Division 4' and 'Matlock Police.' He'd even starred in a few episodes. I'd begun work as a journalist, and, more recently, had a memoir published. Writing quickly became our discussion topic. Jonathon always had a story to tell me, like the time he worked as a 'dresser' for a stage production in London. One evening, he took his break in the car park outside the theatre. A woman approached, and the pair chatted. Betty asked to be remembered to the crew inside the theatre. When Jonathon went back inside, he told the crew Betty had sent her regards. 'But,' replied a crew member, 'Betty's been dead ten years.' Like when Jonathon succumbed to curiosity and entered Melbourne's casino for the one and only time. He put what money he had – two, $1 coins — into a poker machine and pushed the button. Suddenly, bells rang and whistles blew. Then an official appeared, and asked Jonathon to accompany him – to see his prize. He'd won a $50,000 Lexus! At the small memorial service held for Jonathon, I chose not to be gloomy. Instead, I reflected how, at the end of each weekly visit, I would ask Jonathon if I should come back next week. And how, with a beaming smile, he would always reply, *'Oh, yes please.'*

DEAD BOSSES

Thirteen of my former bosses are dead. Reflecting on their deaths gave me pause for thought.

3155 It set me thinking about what kind of people my bosses were. Bosses have the ability to wield serious power over you. That power can manifest itself in a loving way, or in mean and nasty ways. Fortunately, most of my bosses were kind and good people (except probably the farmer who in a fit of rage shot out the radiator in his tractor). As for the others, news of their passing left me feeling sad. One boss was the most gentle man I ever met. He, along with his sons, ran a grazing property in western Victoria. One day, he decided that he and I would muck out the silage pit. It required using the big tractor with its front-end loader (scoop), and a shovel. I was amazed when he told me to hand him the shovel, and for me to do the easy tractor work. I thought the roles should have been reversed. Later, in my fundraising work, I worked mostly for good bosses, where I introduced many school principals to the world of philanthropy and fundraising. After asking a school parent if he would consider giving $50,000 – which he did – the principal and I walked back to our car. On our way, he said to me, 'Now I know why you do what you do.' It was a happy moment from a praising boss. On my first day in another job, my new boss took me to lunch at his favourite (posh) restaurant. Who knows why? On our way in, he introduced me to the maître d', who, all of a sudden, produced a pair of huge scissors from behind his back, and he sliced my boss's tie in half! In another job, the CEO appointed a new, senior manager. The person was an absolute shocker, loved by the CEO but loathed by staff, so much so that *nineteen* people resigned. Six months later, the boss woke up to her, and she was given her marching orders. Then there were my first two newspaper editors, both wonderful people: decent, warm and quick to give praise (or gentle admonishment). I prefer to recall those of my bosses who didn't feel the need to wield their power, even though they had lots of it. As one would expect, almost all of my bosses were older than me; thirteen of them now dead.

WHAT ARE THE ODDS?

In January, 1968, my mother and sister and I were on our way to England.

3156 It was all for my sake. I was to spend twelve months working in our relatives' woollen mills, in England, learning how Australian merino wool was classified, and processed into cloth. The part of the trip we were looking forward to most, before going on to England, was a week's skiing at St Anton, in Austria. As we arrived at the resort, my sister Penny developed a cold so severe; it sent her straight to bed. Nothing, however, was going to stop me. I was quickly on the chairlift, slope-bound. Before I'd completed my first run, however, heavy clouds had moved in, and a blizzard looked ominous. Our hotelier told Mum we should leave immediately, otherwise we might be stuck there, indefinitely. At first light the next morning, we returned to the railway station, only to be told that the tracks heading both east and west already were closed. For a week, at least! A German woman, who'd been hoping to put her car on the train to Zurich, heard Mum's despair. *'You will come with me,'* said Susie. With that, all four of us climbed into Susie's compact VW. It would be a twelve-hour drive. Several times, the VW slid sideways off the winding road into a snow-covered retaining wall. Fortunately, it bounced off each time. We soon discovered Susie (who spoke fluent English) was a freelance journalist, with a PhD in Science. She was also a city councillor. What fascinated us most, though, was that she'd been to Australia, and, among other things, had become friends(!) with a grazier from Mansfield, in north-east Victoria. No, it couldn't be, surely not, my eighteen-year-old brain told myself. This was because four years earlier – I'd spent all of year 10 at our school's bush campus, near Mansfield – it had been common knowledge among us boys that the mother of one boy was in a relationship with a local grazier. Being fourteen, it became the subject of great titillation among us pubescent boys. It was a long day in Susie's car, but eventually, I mustered the courage to suggest a grazier's name. This time, she hit the side barrier a whole lot harder.

ALL ISN'T FINE

It was October, 2004, the day before I was scheduled to have open heart surgery.

3157 I was still dressed, lying on top of my hospital bed, killing time, as they say. A woman whom I guessed to be in her mid-fifties, with neat grey hair and dressed in a matching grey suit, approached. She introduced herself as my surgeon's personal assistant, and proceeded to sit on the chair next to my bedhead. Fleetingly, my brain pondered why a surgeon would have a personal assistant, let alone one who did hospital rounds on a Sunday afternoon. But I let it pass. 'How are you?' she asked. I freely admitted to feeling fragile. Open heart surgery is a worry at any time, and I was scared. I glanced around, looking for paperwork she might have brought with her, but there was none. My lower lip began to quiver, and I placed my hand over my mouth. 'I'm fine,' I replied, lying. She looked at me. 'Do you know what fine means?' she asked. What was going on here? I thought. 'Tell me,' I answered. '*Fucked-up, Insecure, Neurotic, Egotistical*,*' she said, without missing a beat. With that, she stood, said goodbye, and left. I never saw the woman again. People to whom I've told this story asked me why I didn't say something — or complain — to my surgeon. Complain to my surgeon? Would he admit to having a whacky PA, one who did Sunday rounds — and who swore? Would not my very questioning of him be impertinent? I decided to be silent. Sixteen years later, it remains a mystery. But, I wager that whenever someone tells you they are fine, you'll put a wry grin on your face. (*attributed to Canadian crime writer Louise Penny)

NO NUMBER, NO NAME

This entry has no number and no name; it concerns my alcoholic father

no number Mum threw him out when I was five, and he fell over a hotel balcony and died when I was thirteen. A father is not supposed to do that; he is supposed to teach his son to be a man, and to do manly things. I resent it hugely that my father was never there for me.

VOCATION

3158 *At times I wish I had used my fundraising skills not in education but for real needs.*

*

Among what I experienced were two year ten kids, who gave $4 towards a new learning hub

*

The 'tea lady' where I worked gave $5, saying, 'Michael, I hope this is enough'

*

Two parents in business together each gave $20,000 — because I asked them

*

A parent said he'd give $50,000 providing we didn't tell his wife

A university alumnus gave $90,000 over three years to fund a PhD student

*

A past student told me he was putting the college in his will for $100,000; two days later, after we had met, he phoned to say he'd increased his future bequest to $250,000

*

A parent sat through a fundraising lunch looking decidedly unhappy; he then gave $100,000

*

A family gave $500,000 — and guaranteed the full amount of their gift in their joint wills

*

A couple gave $1,000,000 — they also guaranteed the full amount in their wills

*

A family with no prior connection to the school first made me check its bona fides (by calling another school, and then another) — they ended up giving $2,000,000

*

CORONAVIRUS PANDEMIC

The coronavirus deaths have been horrific; so terribly sad. So many deaths. So much sadness.

3159 we all feel for the families of those who died. We feel for the family members who, because of distancing rules imposed, were not allowed to be with their family member before and while they passed away. Our thoughts and prayers have been and remain with them all.

THE GOOD

COVID-19 has brought out the best and the worst in people. Let's start with the best:

3160 the virus should be named 'The Wenliang Virus' in honour of the courageous Chinese ophthalmologist, Dr Li Wenliang, who alerted the world to the virus on 30 December 2019, blew the whistle on the virus, was reprimanded by state authorities for 'rumour-mongering', and later died from the virus. He was thirty-four, and he should not be forgotten

3161 the wonderful, frontline, medical staff: doctors, nurses, researchers, cleaners, indeed all associated with a health system, who battled so hard to save lives during the pandemic

3162 the chief medical officers and all those who worked in the background to make good things happen — and who tried to keep us calm

3163 the selfless, wonderfully generous folk who performed amazing acts of kindness to fellow Australians throughout the pandemic

3164 the lone shopper who said to the elderly lady in the supermarket queue, *'You are my granny for the day and I want to pay for your groceries'*

3165 the woman who paid for the next sixty customers' coffees

3166 the man who paid for the next fifteen customers' pizzas

3167 the café owner who withdrew $5,000 from his bank and handed it out in 'lettuce-leaf' $100 notes to fifty people standing in a queue outside a Centrelink branch

3168 the wonderful nurse who, after clocking-off from her 12-hour shift, returned to the ward to sit with her patient while he died

3169 the 90-year-old woman in Belgium who refused a ventilator, telling her doctor, *'I've had a good life; give it to a younger patient'*

3170 the Brooklyn (USA) landlord who waived the rent for all 80 tenants

3171 the Baker's Delight franchisee which at day's end gave a charity worker two big bags of bread rolls, then went and put together another five bags

3172 due to the STAY AT HOME rules, Australians saved $38 million per day on poker machine losses

3173 people who went onto their apartment balcony at night to applaud frontline workers

3174 the woman upstairs who gave me her copy of *The Age*

3175 the Qantas pilot who reinvented himself as a proud Coles check out person

3176 not everyone said they wanted to return to their pre-coronavirus lifestyle

3177 Defence Force job applications rose by 40 per cent during the pandemic (37,000 applications in one month); young people sought job security

3178 cask wine tasted better during lockdown

THE BAD

3179 the 'Aspen (skiing) Group,' which ignored isolation edicts, partied, and played golf

3180 the arrogant, entitled, despicable, reckless dinner party groups

3181 the terrorists who 'blew-up' a hospital's IT systems

3182 the US preacher who refused to stop holding full-on church services, who said to the state governor, *'Your jurisdiction ends at my church door'*

3183 couples which broke up over differing attitudes to isolation rules

3184 large sums of money allocated to combat domestic violence during isolation

3185 the 16,000 Australians who decided to travel overseas in defiance of the highest level government advice

3186 the man in compulsory isolation in Perth, who left his hotel several times, on one occasion travelling by public transport to visit his girlfriend (he was caught, charged and denied bail)

3187 people not allowed into Queensland to see a dying parent, while actors and business and sporting 'celebrities' were allowed to walk straight in without being quarantined

3188 retailers who price-gouged customers — because they could during the upheaval

3189 the billionaire retail giant who said the virus was good for his business

3190 the recently-returned overseas tourists who whinged about having to spend 14 days in isolation in Melbourne's hotels

3191 the president of Brazil who said, *'Everyone has to die sometime'*

3192 the lowlife who stole groceries straight out of a blind shopper's trolley

3193 the cyclist who deliberately coughed in the face of the TV cameraman as he rode past

3194 bogans who abused supermarket staff

3195 the group of millennials who regularly held parties in our apartment block

3196 the poor, elderly pensioner couple who left the supermarket empty handed after being scared half-to-death by aggressive, feral shoppers

3197 bogan shoppers early in the pandemic filmed fighting over toilet paper

3198 one has to wonder if the cruise ship industry will recover; would you go on a cruise?

3199 sports' administrators — they know who they are — who put money ahead of human life; zero respect, zero health and safety, zero support, zero integrity, zero brains

3200 private schools might need to rethink building Olympic standard swimming pools

3201 unbelievable news that universities will continue to receive the same level of federal funding regardless of the decline in student numbers

3202 retailers who scared the elderly with unnecessary telemarketing 'offers'

3203 the lowlife who licked a line of deodorant cans on a supermarket shelf (his lawyer argued in court that his client wasn't really a bad person)

3204 the group of campers on the riverbank, who'd been told to STAY AT HOME

3205 people who were still being caught holding dinner parties

3206 8,000 businesses dobbed in for allegedly rorting JobKeeper, including having 2,200 employees on multiple applications for payments

3207 the Ukraine church leader who said coronavirus was God's punishment for same-sex marriage himself caught COVID-19

3208 death threats made to lawmakers who passed strict lockdown laws

3209 the business leader who said some people needed to die from COVID-19 so shareholders could get their rightful dividends

3210 the second waves were inevitable

3211 did you get as angry as I did at the selfish idiots who flaunted lockdown rules?

3212 the supermarket chain which introduced pre-booked queue-jumping shopping to make the average punter who waited quietly in line really annoyed

3213 the AFL season would have been cactus the moment one player, official or hub resident family member tested positive for coronavirus, but didn't

3214 the numbers of Americans who died from COVID-19 equalled three full passenger aircraft falling from the skies *every day*

3215 one could understand America's coronavirus death rate under a truly incompetent, thick leader, but one cannot excuse Britain's appalling statistic in a once-brilliant country

3216 during lockdown, 200 people attended an unlawful party at Jindabyne NSW; 100 fled before police were able to issue crowd limitation fines

3217 the smart-arsed female who joked on FB about fooling police at state border check point; people called for her to be fined, jailed, whipped, made to tour an ICU ward, and then forced to do 10,000 hours of community work for the police officer's charity of choice

3218 If, during COVID-19 you didn't attend your holiday home in 60 days, your insurance policy might now be void

3219 thirty-year-olds who accessed the full government allowed coronavirus super drawdown of $20,000 are likely to have foregone $120,000 in super capital when they retire

3220 reports that Amazon owner's wealth increased by A$52 billion during the pandemic

3221 consider the single mum who welcomed the 'ISO' lockdown during COVID-19 because it meant she no longer had to make yet another excuse why she couldn't afford to take her kids out for dinner

3222 according to the government minister responsible, a booze barn in Melbourne's CBD capable of serving close to 1,000 drinkers was able to open during coronavirus lockdown without serving food or keeping social distancing because it was a place ... wait for it, *'of major cultural importance to the state'* — can you believe it?

3223 why couldn't a UK prime minister who oversaw 40,000+ coronavirus deaths in his country simply say *'I'm sorry'*?

3224 why couldn't a US president who oversaw

250,000+ coronavirus deaths in his country simply say *'I'm sorry'*

3225 COVID-19 proved to be a pragmatic and legal way for bosses to off-load staff they'd long wished they could shed, but hitherto couldn't do so legally without due cause

3226 10,000+ Victorians refused to be tested for COVID-19

3227 four-fifths of superannuants were anxious about the diminished value of their super fund following coronavirus

3228 constantly overtaken when entering the supermarket by shoppers of all ages rushing in without pausing to use the complimentary hand sanitiser

3229 what kind of world do we live in when a COVID-19 testing station needed to display a sign saying 'Aggressive behaviour will not be tolerated?' Are we really that primitive a people?

3230 thousands of Britons flocked to beaches during COVID-19 against medical advice

3231 Briton's peak medical body called for a non-accusatory national forward-thinking coronavirus strategy plan, but Boris said no

3232 millennials who got blamed for spreading coronavirus

3233 is it true the CovidSafe app didn't work if your

phone was turned off and locked, which many phones are when they are not actually in use?

3234 COVID-19 outbreaks at a government favoured meat works, security guards having sex with people they were supposed to be supervising in hotel quarantine, nursing home mis-treatment and other disasters — all appalling mis-management

3235 is it sheer naivety to hope we might have come out of coronavirus a kinder, more considerate, more tolerant, more compassionate society? hardly likely

3236 after eight months of pandemic lockdown, going just about anywhere to do just about anything with just about anyone for just about any reason sounds ultra-compelling

3237 a surfer broke lockdown rules to look for better waves

3238 abattoirs told meat workers not to take time out to be tested for COVID-19 because it would mess with shift rosters

3239 stage 4 total lockdown included an 8 pm–5 am curfew; a curfew in Australia? unbelievable

3240 1.42 million COVID-19 deaths worldwide (as at December 2020) one death every fifteen seconds

3241 two men arrested for planning a Sunday street march during Stage FOUR in our State of Disaster; another who drove out after curfew to buy cigarettes

3242 with nineteen deaths overnight in Victoria, anti-maskers should have been herded into a sealed room with five volunteer 'positives' — and given time, like a month, to reflect on their gross ignorance and stupidity

3243 the high school student who resented putting the saving of lives above her generation's future financial prospects forgot to consider her ageing grandparents

3244 more than 2.6 million Australians dipped into their superannuation during COVID-19, withdrawing $27 billion

3245 the young and not so young who prayed they would catch the virus — as a way out of their mental despair

3246 far-right newspaper journalist: *'Old people are going to die anyway'*

3247 never a worse time to try to lease or sell office space

3248 never a worse time for actors and artists

3249 the woman who tweeted that COVID-19 *'wasn't killing men fast enough'* - she received a huge arts grant from Melbourne City Council

THE FUNNY

Without intending for one moment to minimise the tragedy which occurred to grieving families, research shows that even a faint dose of humour was able to ease stress ...

3250 the bright spark who wrote, 'They said a mask and gloves were enough to go to the supermarket; they lied: everyone else wore clothes' (I repeat)

3251 country folk who set up a hugely oversized mouse trap, with a roll of toilet paper in the spot where you'd normally put the cheese

3252 the guy at Coles who got berated by a shopper for having a trolley full of the same item; he replied to the angry shopper, 'That's all good, mate, but I work here; do you mind if I carry on filling the shelves?'

3253 we can no longer use 'having-to-run' as an excuse to end a phone call

3254 'Hi, I'm a reporter. Are you the landlord who yesterday evicted a tenant who was unable to pay her rent? I don't want to interview you; I want to smack you in the face.'

3255 US TV host Chris Cuomo saying (on air) to his brother Andrew Cuomo, governor of New York state, 'You need to call our mother; there's always time to call your mother.' To which Andrew replied, 'I just did call her; she said I was her favourite!'

3256 in a reversal of normal practice, a teenager yelled at his parents for going out

3257 I stepped onto our bathroom scales; it said, 'Please use social distancing: one at a time'

3258 people who, during the pandemic, were doing fake commutes: i.e. going for a drive as if they were going to work, then returning home to begin the working day from home

3259 sign: 'If you enter our store without a mask we will need to take your temperature — and we have only rectal thermometers'

3260 Zoom overuse during pandemic lockdown led to record numbers of women seeking plastic surgery

3261 hub or bubble? What's it matter — all expenses are paid anyway

3262 I said that when COVID-19 was over, I was going to hug everyone so much it would be weird

3263 (news report) Dutch government urged single people to adopt a sex buddy during pandemic lockdown

3264 Barcelona opera house reopened after coronavirus with a concert for 2,292 potted plants

3265 to where will it be safe to travel post COVID-19?

3266 a guy said his mother-in-law's stew was bland and tasteless, so she phoned the COVID-19 hotline and had him put into quarantine for 14 days

3267 feeling for people who relied on lip-reading while everyone was wearing a face mask

3268 amazing to think how we once ate birthday cake after someone blew all over it

3269 sales of sex toys were up by 30% during the pandemic lockdown

EPILOGUE

3270 people who continue to deny the pandemic was real

3271 still hugely worried for young families with massive mortgages, when interest rates return from their present all-time low, even to the 17% they were at when I was their age

3272 what's to stop a COVID-22 or 27 or 31 — one ten times worse than COVID-19?

3273 post coronavirus, will the millennials really wage war against us baby boomers?

3274 with due respect, were you to find errors, duplications or typos in this book, they are all deliberately included to piss you off

3275 readers must understand that the writer has a vast number of peculiarities

3276 I seriously worry about what I will do when my superannuation fund runs out

3277 I repeat: '*Never give in, never give in; never, never, never, never*' (Churchill)

3278 I spent countless hours getting this numbering correct — I just hope you appreciate it

3279 it's kind of levelling and encouraging to know that Steve Jobs studied Shakespeare, calligraphy and modern dance [not IT or commerce]

3280 as I write, the cricket season has begun, BUT One Day Internationals (ODIs) are NOT being broadcast on free-to-air TV; this is outrageous, and it pisses me off something awful

3281 the safer place for a peaceful and more stable future would be Byron Bay or Taiwan?

3282 every time I sip my evening whisky I think of my late ex-father-in-law, who always insisted we had a refill (his shout); such a wise and sensible and generous man

3283 sometimes, life is like a martini but without the olive

3284 have you ever wondered how many trees it takes to print a year's worth of your favourite sales catalogue/newspaper?

3285 'All-You-Can-Eat' restaurants and patrons with eyes bigger than stomachs

3286 the same 'All-You-Can-Eat' restaurant where a

young obese couple next to us asked for more dishes than would fit on their table

3287 men who sit with their knees wide apart

3288 young men who believe aggression defines manliness

3289 winners have parties, losers have meetings

3290 I'm not a busybody or into gossip, but did you hear about the latest sportsman who posted pics of his privates on social media?

3291 why are all of my doctors so damn knowledgeable?

3292 cricket commentator implies concussion is self-inflicted: *'it was his own fault'*

3293 would 'Vietnam' have happened had JFK not been shot?

3294 report: Mexico wants to pay for the wall

3295 report: Canada wants a wall, too

3296 report: North Korean dictator declares: 'I no longer craziest leader'

3297 I will have the choice of two last resort defences should litigation eventuate from all of this: (1) 'Only joking!' or (2) 'Get stuffed!'; take your pick

3298 having to eat humble pie

3299 damn it; I woke up again this morning

3300 this too shall pass

no number happy holidays

FEEDBACK

Feel welcome to send your gripes to ... michaelthorntonbooks@gmail.com — and be nice!

LEFTOVERS

a leftovers which are left uneaten
b report: Jenny never liked Melania, either
c idiots who drive at speed on flooded roads
d idiots who swim outside the flags
e idiots who dice with death
f 'On Sale' prices which are dearer than normal
g why would you pay a fortune to an advertising agency for a TV ad (for ginger beer) which contains incorrect English spoken by a man who should know better?
h people who say MCG when they mean MCC
i I don't want stupid points; I want cheaper prices
j Sunday is the first day of the week, not the last
k pizza, burger, bucket and drink ads with far bigger portions than you get when you go to the store
l our daily sales catalogue still has a few pages set aside for news of the day
m sad when people you've helped ignore you when

you are no longer of any use to them (not that you were looking for any reward, just courtesy)

n   I know I'm slowing down, but I'm trying to hide it from my family

o   the nation's leader decides to keep his overseas holiday a secret from us; what does that say about truly important decisions he's required to make?

p   I'm gobsmacked how with only three apartments sharing our new (purple) 'glass-only' recycle bin, in the bin's first two weeks of operation the other two households filled the bin to capacity with more than one hundred beer stubbies

q   'Googleink', 'loomink' and singleink' all in one radio broadcast

r   be honest, there are (at least) two Australias: one which gardens and belongs to book clubs, another which racially taunts foreign cricketers (rudely asking a player how many wives he has)

s   in his debut Test, a batsman twice swings wildly and misses, and the commentator says he has settled into his innings *'nicely'*

t   Facebook owns Instagram, Google owns YouTube; I own a set of whiteboard markers

u   report: thirteen of the twenty-two members of the federal cabinet are said to have a connection to Hillsong Church; scary, isn't it?

v   interviews on *The Project*, where I don't understand a single word said

w   one day someone will walk into your life and you will realise why it never worked before

x   white delivery vans (they always drive like maniacs)

y   *'Kingston Town can't win'* (it did)

z   SUV ads on TV which show vehicles hooning in the outback, when 99.9% of SUVs never leave Toorak, Darling Point, Teneriffe, Unley Park, Dalkeith or Battery Point

--- **ends** ---

www.ingramcontent.com/pod-product-compliance
Lightning Source LLC
Chambersburg PA
CBHW021137080526
44588CB00008B/103